Calling
Church & Seminary
into the 21st Century

Calling
Church & Seminary into the 21st Century

Donald E. Messer

Abingdon Press
Nashville

CALLING CHURCH & SEMINARY INTO THE 21ST CENTURY

Library of Congress Cataloging-in-Publication Data

Messer, Donald E.
    Calling church and seminary into the 21st century / Donald E. Messer.
        p.   cm.
    Includes bibliographical references and index.
    ISBN 0-687-01351-8 (alk. paper)
        1. Theology—Study and teaching—United States.   2. Theological
seminaries—United States—History—20th century.   3. Oden, Thomas C.
Requiem.   I. Title.
BV4030.M47   1995
207'.1'1—dc20   95-12001
                                                                                CIP

To

My sister, Rose Marie
and
My brother-in-law, LeRoy Mutschelknaus
and their sons
David George
Brad Emil
John Alan
and
Scott Donald

CONTENTS

FOREWORD

The introduction to a book should be the same as the introduction of a speaker: Be brief, provide data pertinent to the author and topic, and offer brief hints of what is to follow. It also helps if one knows the author. I am so blessed, for I have known and appreciated the work of Don Messer since we first met on a warm South Dakota morning in the summer of 1969. He had only recently arrived home from his graduate studies in Boston to begin his ministry in a local church. I was the speaker at a conference pastors' school. Don's bishop had told me to be sure and meet this young man. "He's smart, dedicated and he will play an important role in the future of this church."

I found Don sitting on the grass outside the conference center, reading. He had no intention of interrupting his morning reading to listen to this particular visiting lecturer, whose topic I now forget, but which was obviously not appealing enough to attract young Don Messer. I suspect at the time I was offended that he would miss the chance to listen to me. But what I also remember is that he was gracious, polite, and firm in his decision to keep reading. The politic thing to have done was to have made a courtesy call in the lecture hall and then to have slipped out at the first opportunity.

An older Don Messer might have done the politic thing, but I liked the authenticity of that young pastor-scholar. That summer encounter in South Dakota sums up Don Messer for me: He is a scholar with a pastoral vision, and a person who is centered in his determination to give his best in serving God and his church as he has done as pastor and as college and seminary administrator.

This book is Don Messer's call to action to mainline Protestantism and its theological seminaries. In that call, he argues that both church and seminary must listen to their critics, reflect on their shortcomings, and then push forward with a determination to meet a 21st century challenge that accepts methodological changes with the same fervor with which it remains faithful to the traditional gospel message.

The politic thing to do in looking at the mainline church's critics would be to evade specificity. Don Messer believes—and this becomes clear in this book—that dialogue demands that we talk to one another openly. He identifies Thomas Oden's recent writings as a prime example of what he calls an assault on the seminaries. He correctly identifies the attacks as an issue of political control. While his primary focus is on his own United Methodist denomination, he insists that the internal struggle with political critics is being conducted across the ecumenical spectrum.

Messer knows the shortcomings and limitations of the church's seminaries, and he knows the shortsightedness of its local parishes. He also knows the strengths and wisdom of both the academy and the parish. Between the two there is an inevitable tension because they have different assignments and different goals. But as the scripture reminds us: "What then is Apollos? What is Paul? Servants through whom you believed, as the Lord assigned to each. I planted, Apollos watered, but God gave the growth. . . . So neither he who plants nor he who waters is anything, but only God who gives the growth" (1 Corinthians 3:5-7). The local church and the seminary classroom are different locales with the same task: to plant and water so that God may give the growth.

But as Messer wisely counsels, for growth to take place through the mechanism of our human limitations, the church and its seminary components must remain sensitive to change and faithful to tradition, without succumbing to a political struggle that oversimplifies the ambiguity and complexity that have been an inevitable part of the religious community's life since Abraham departed on his journey from Ur.

This book calls us to accept the reality of our internal conflicts but to acknowledge that we have only limited worldviews in our church and seminary communities. What we do in those communities must always be measured against God's call, which John Wesley reminded us involves both heart and mind.

Anti-intellectualism, and fear of change—and that is what is finally at the heart of this conflict—is not new to American life. To reflect on the nature of being, much less than on the nature of the church, is to risk hearing new ways of addressing complex issues. In that assignment, we are limited by our placement in time and space. We must deal with that limitation by risking ourselves with bold new efforts within the framework of the biblical tradition, as Don Messer so cogently reminds us throughout this book. We will fail to be so engaged if we allow our internal debate over the future of the church and its seminaries to disintegrate into a battle over power politics.

Even as we plan for the future we must also listen to the past. In looking back, we will hear words that are prophetic and demand our current attention. Don Messer found such words addressed to an earlier troubled period in American life by U.S. Senator Robert F. Kennedy, who told a crowd in Indianapolis on the night that Martin Luther King, Jr., was assassinated: "What we need...is not division;...not hatred;... not violence or lawlessness, but love and wisdom, and compassion toward one another, and the feeling of justice toward those who still suffer."

It is in this spirit that Don Messer has addressed the conflict and the challenge facing the church and its seminaries as they prepare to enter the 21st century.

James M. Wall

A United Methodist clergyperson, James M. Wall has been editor of the *Christian Century* magazine since 1972.

"In deserto parate viam Domini,
rectas facite in solitudine
semitas Dei nostri."
Liber Isiae 40:3

"Parate viam Domini,
rectas facite semitas eius."
Evangelium secundum Lucam 3:4

PREFACE

Today in the United States we take for granted the presence of graduate theological schools preparing persons for Christian ministry and other forms of religious and professional leadership. In reality seminaries are unique institutions in American life. The need for higher education enterprises committed to critical and creative theological teaching, scholarship, and research was not always self-evident to the church, and the services these enterprises render to church and society were not always welcomed.

In frontier America, for example, learning and piety sometimes were viewed as being antithetical and seminary education was considered unnecessary. The "call of God" often was viewed as the only requirement for effective ministry. Opponents of theological education like Peter Cartwright said that preachers trained in schools were as pale as "lettuce growing under the shade of a peach tree," and their preaching as awkward as "a gosling that had got the straddles by wading in the dew."[1] Such frontier anti-intellectualism, however, did not prevent visionary Christian leaders throughout the country from overcoming overwhelming obstacles to establish seminaries "for the better preparation and education of persons called to the high and holy office of the Christian ministry."[2]

Tensions Between Churches and Seminaries

Seminaries typically experience tension in their relationships with their church constituencies. Theoretically, the church wants to be in touch with the best thinking each generation of intellectuals offers, but feelings fluctuate when these thoughts challenge age-old doctrines and dogmas or individual professors take stances contrary to popular and established beliefs. Seminaries officially proclaim they seek to be servants of the church, but the temptation at times to bow and be recognized before the altars of academia may lead to alienation or, at least, an apparent drifting away from the faith community that has established and encouraged their existence.

Sometimes "rocky" relationships and marriages consist of couples who cannot seem to live with each other but also cannot seem to endure without each other. People sometimes have almost a "love-hate" relationship. Likewise churches and seminaries occasionally lapse into such patterns of attitude and behavior. A church will establish a seminary—even express pride in its existence and service—but then starve it financially. Or a seminary will gladly accept the church's resources, but then stiff-arm a congregation's request for pastoral assistance. Finding and maintaining a healthy relationship of caring and criticizing between the two proves to be a continuous and problematic process.

A Synopsis of This Book

In the chapters ahead, I have attempted to limit the possible themes, yet be inclusive of the primary concerns imperative in the dialogue of critical lovers of the contemporary seminary. The first chapter explores the purposes and priorities of the seminaries in relation to the church. Amid the struggle for the soul of the church, the seminaries serve as intellectual centers, yet are not immune from the political battle. The primary focus, however, must be on emphasizing the call to Christian ministry as the most overpaid profession in the world!

"The New Assault on the Seminaries" is examined in chapter 2, with special attention to responding to the criticisms raised by Thomas C. Oden in his book *Requiem: A Lament in Three Movements.*[3] Chapter 3 acknowledges that "the future ain't what it used to be," and, therefore, the changing canons of culture—multiracial, multicultural, multireligious pluralism—necessitate new visions of the vocation of the seminaries. Though theological schools are fundamentally and inherently conservative institutions, the fourth chapter contends that the faithful transmission of God's Word has a subversive quality. Academic freedom challenges the political correctness of both left and right. Conflict and controversy are inevitable consequences of prophetic, dynamic institutions seeking to be on the cutting edge of theological inquiry and the geography of faith.

A vision of the seminary as a redemptive community constitutes the core of chapter 5. The pastoral functions of theological education are accented in discussions on knowing and caring. Envisioning new seminary curriculums and policies is needed. In the sixth chapter, I suggest a new paradigm of "publish *and* parish" rather than the old but truthful cliché of "publish *or* perish." Both clergy and faculty are challenged to abandon the "either/or" choice of "publish" and "parish," searching for ways to find a better balance between scholarship and service, theoretical and practical, academic and parish life. Chapter 7 explores what the new information superhighway may mean for both the church and seminary of the twenty-first century. Pastors don't just ride the circuit anymore, but plug into cyberspace via fax machines, satellite television, electronic mail, the internet, and other forms of electronic communication. Seminary education in the future will transcend distance, offering courses such as the electronic lectionary to rural places in the United States as well as other parts of the globe. In an age of "cyberfaith," the new world of communications opens new avenues for education and evangelism.

A brief bibliography at the end is intended to encourage readers to explore in greater depth the issues related to theological education. It also acknowledges my debt of gratitude to those who have probed these questions in the past and have provided us with a rich resource of reflection and insight. This book, unlike most others on ministerial education, focuses not on professional theological educators but on an audience of clergy and laity who faithfully support and count on the seminaries for intellectual assistance and theological leadership.

This book recognizes that since the 1980s Christian theological educators of various persuasions have been engaged in an extensive and thoughtful debate about theological schooling. Theologian David H. Kelsey has outlined and critiqued the various contributors to this substantive discussion in his book *Between Athens and Berlin: The Theological Education Debate.*[4] These include the contributions of Edward Farley, Max L. Stackhouse, John B. Cobb, Jr., Joseph C. Hough, Jr., Charles M. Wood, Katie G. Cannon, and others. The interested reader is invited to read these and other authors listed in the selected bibliography of this book. Unfortunately, this dialogue has been confined to seminary faculties and administrators, and the church has not been an active participant.[5] This book hopefully serves as a partial bridge between this debate among theological educators and the broader community of Christian faith.

Special Words of Appreciation

It is especially to these laity and clergy that I owe very special words of appreciation. Since first being ordained in The United Methodist Church more than thirty years ago, my life has been greatly enriched by close association with a caring and compassionate Christian community, both locally and globally. I have great faith in the good judgment of rank-and-file church members and leaders. Extremists of both left and right, for their own political purposes, may attempt to distort the history of their churches and the record of their seminaries, but ultimately the wise and prudent common sense of the middle majority prevails.

Over the years I have been especially blessed to be associated with progressive Christian laity and clergy who have served as college and seminary trustees. For almost twenty-five years I have had the privilege of being president of institutions (first

Dakota Wesleyan University and now The Iliff School of Theology) that have had governing boards dominated by at least two-thirds laity. Far from being status quo oriented or fearful of change, they have been visionary critical lovers who have generously contributed their energies and resources to enhance the future welfare of their church and its schools. They have never let immediate problems or even temporary controversies dissuade them from pursuing long-range dreams and agendas that they believed would enhance the mission, ministry, and leadership of Christ's church.

Special gratitude is due to the trustees of The Iliff School of Theology for a study leave that enabled me to complete this manuscript. A break from administrative responsibilities was only possible because of the willingness of administrative and faculty colleagues to take on extra duties. Thanks are especially due to Delwin Brown for serving as acting chief executive officer, and to Jane I. Smith, Thomas K. Craine, Sally B. Geis, James W. McGillivray, and Sara J. Myers for their outstanding staff support. Student research assistance was ably provided by Catherine Whitlatch. Alberta Smith, as executive secretary to the president, not only managed the office, but also assisted with this manuscript.

Many of the ideas appearing in this manuscript have been critiqued by various publics. Primary among them have been faculty, trustees, alumni, and students of The Iliff School of Theology. Other audiences have included the Minnesota Consortium of Theological Schools, The Boston University School of Theology Alumni Association, the Eastern Pennsylvania United Methodist Annual Conference, the World Division of the United Methodist Board of Global Ministries, United Methodist Conference Boards of Ministry, and various local Colorado churches. Service as president of the Association of United Methodist Theological Schools (1990–92), membership on the United Methodist University Senate, and on accrediting teams of the North Central Association of Colleges and Universities have helped broaden my views on excellence in theological education. Opportunities to consult in Nepal and lecture in South Korea and Guatemala, as well as visits to seminaries in Brazil, Argentina,

Poland, Germany, England, Russia, and China have helped broaden my perspectives on theological education.

Editorial review of the complete manuscript was provided by Delwin Brown, Sally B. Geis, Bonnie J. Messer, and Paul Murphy. Janet Fishburn, Robin W. Lovin, and Neal F. Fisher critiqued short sections. To each I owe deep appreciation, but none of them bears any responsibility for the final draft of this document. When writing a book, critical editors are indeed an author's best friends!

Love and appreciation also must be expressed to my family who has endured not only the writing of this book but the many years of church, administrative and public life reflected in it. My wife, Bonnie, and our children, Christine and Kent, always have been my most loving critics! Together, with our son-in-law, Gordon, we enjoy a special relationship that I treasure beyond any words that I can express.

CHAPTER ONE

How Are They to Hear without a Preacher?

How are they to hear without a preacher? And how can people preach unless they are sent? As it is written, "How beautiful are the feet of those who bring good news!"

ROMANS 10:14-15

Not long ago I was invited to an ordination. As I approached St. John's Episcopal Cathedral in Denver, a feeling of discomfort overwhelmed me as I remembered the last Episcopal ordination I had attended. Despite its traditional beauty and meaningful liturgy, the memory of the young African American man being required to lie prostrate before the white bishop had left within me a bitter distaste. How unseemly it felt in light of historic racism both inside and outside the church.

Though excited that my woman friend was to be ordained a priest, I dreaded the moment when she too would be commanded to lie flat on the floor before a male bishop. Such images of authority and obedience appear inappropriate within the church after centuries of sexism. Imagine then my surprise and joy, when the ordaining bishop in a special ceremony did not ask her to lie submissively prostrate but instead knelt down himself and kissed her feet.

By word and deed the bishop proclaimed a theological understanding of servanthood inherent in the nature of Christian ministry. In my mind, he validated his authority as a Christian leader by demonstrating qualities of authentic humility, graciousness, and service. He overcame hierarchical distance by assuming the posture of Jesus kneeling to wash the feet of his disciples. When he kissed her feet, the bishop reminded us of the centrality of Jesus as a caring salvific figure in human history who shapes decisively the portrait of Christian ministry throughout the ages.[1]

Likewise, theological schools are called to be servants of a servant God. A seminary that distances itself from the church is like a bishop demanding that an ordinand lie prostrate. A seminary caught up in its own hierarchical self-importance has forgotten to Whom it witnesses and for Whom it exists.

Preparation of Preachers

Three basic purposes are fundamental to the vocational calling of a theological school.[2] *The first and fundamental task of the seminary is to ensure there are effective clergy and lay preachers to proclaim the gospel of God's love in Jesus Christ.* With rare exceptions, the primary purpose of most graduate professional theological schools is the preparation of pastors, priests, diaconal ministers, educators, missionaries, and so forth. Within that context seminaries seek to accent four basic goals: (1) acquiring and transmitting theological knowledge, (2) developing professional skill, (3) promoting personal and social growth, and (4) deepening of Christian commitment and service through spiritual formation. When this mission is accomplished effectively, future generations inevitably will say again as of old: "How beautiful are the feet of those who bring good news!"

The bold innovation in the ordination service reminded me of the concept of beautiful feet as articulated in the book of Isaiah and in Paul's Letter to the Romans. Few of us think of our feet as being beautiful; most of us consider our feet ugly. Our gnarled and twisted toes, our calluses and corns, our dirt and sweat, are not exactly aesthetic objects. Functionally, however, our feet can be considered divine. For it is the life and message that our feet bear that makes the difference between beauty and unsightliness.

In Isaiah 52:7-12, the prophet is so transported in thought that in a poetic outburst he describes the coming joy and exultation of the people of Jerusalem when they learn that God has returned to Zion and that God's people have made the long march home from their Babylonian captivity. The prophet saw beauty in the feet of the messenger who declared God's victory and Israel's salvation. Beautiful are the feet of one who publishes peace, who announces the good news of deliverance. Beautiful are the feet of one who publishes peace, who announces the restoration of harmony within the community. How beautiful upon the mountains are the feet of one who declares the salvation and safety of Israel.

Paul picked up this unusual theme in his writings to the Romans. Concerned about the extension of Christ's message through mission and evangelism, he asks four key questions:

But how are they to call on one in whom they have not believed? And how are they to believe in one of whom they have never heard? And how are they to hear without someone to proclaim him? And how are they to proclaim him unless they are sent? (Romans 10:14-15)

Then Paul responds by citing Isaiah: "How beautiful are the feet of those who bring good news!"

Feet are being presented as a metaphor, not as a literal, physical requirement. Many persons in this world cannot for various reasons use their feet for walking or running. For example, just before Christmas in 1992, Darryl Fairchild, an outstanding young Ph.D. student at The Iliff School of Theology suffered permanent paralysis due to a highly unusual bicycle accident. I certainly would understand if he despaired and cried out against the personal injustice in God's creation, but instead he has continued to live out the gospel in caring and pastoral ways. His home congregation in Ohio was spiritually overwhelmed when he triumphantly returned to preach in a wheelchair a few months after the accident. Truly, Paul continues to ask, "How can they hear without a preacher?" and Isaiah paraphrased would read, "How beautiful are the *wheels* of those who bring good news!"

Education of the *Laos* for Ministry

The education of the total people of God, the laos *for ministry, represents the second major missional purpose of the seminary.* Lest there be any misunderstanding when I speak of seminaries existing "for the better preparation and education of persons called to the high and holy office of the Christian ministry," I do not construe seminary education as the sole province of clergy. Reference to the "high and holy office" probably historically meant clergy, but a renewed understanding of the ministry of the *laos,* the whole people of God, affirms theological education for all. Recognizing that Christian ministry is for all of God's people, most seminaries do not restrict their educational offerings and opportunities just to those who are preparing for "professional" leadership.

In fact, the hunger for theological education extends beyond the baptized and believers. Craig Dykstra of the Lilly Endowment has noted that "people are asking questions about God; and they yearn for coherent, thoughtful guidance as well as fresh access to the deep veins of wisdom that at least some of them suspect are still there to be mined from historical religious traditions." Increasingly, seminaries are being discovered by persons outside the established church who are engaging in spiritual journeys. Dykstra suggests that the hunger for theological education is in response to "a fundamental human need." Thus "theological education in its full sense is not just for some but for all."[3]

Theologian Edward Farley of The Divinity School of Vanderbilt University has cautioned against the "clergy paradigm" or clerical captivity of theological education. Theological schooling is more than preparing persons for "successful" clerical practice or leadership. Clergy education is not unimportant, but it does not fully encompass the purpose or goal of theological education. The functions clergy perform should not solely determine the objectives and content of the seminaries. As Kelsey observes:

> The point here is not to denigrate the importance of educating clergy; nor is it to deny that education of clergy is embraced by theological education. Rather, it is to urge that the end to which theological education is ordered, whatever it may be, is an end that

24

is basic to the well-being of far more walks of life than just the peculiar calling of the clergy. . . . We cannot achieve the education of superlative church leaders by a course of study defined by the roles and tasks of church leadership.[4]

Thus the whole church has a stake in the future of theological education. It not only forms and transforms those in clerical leadership positions but helps shape the ministry of the laity. A vital and vibrant church needs a seminary community devoted to a faith within whose heritage and future the advancement of wisdom and learning continues to be integral. A vital and vibrant seminary needs the historic and contemporary ethical and religious vision and vitality of the church. The seminary stands as a bridge between the church and academia, inviting both to journey across in the quest for truth.

Therefore, theological education at its best almost always has been rooted in scholarly, academic communities. A school of theology should be a center for the church's theological life. It was the school of theology at Alexandria where the mind of the church first encountered and incorporated the spirit of Hellenism. The theological schools of Cologne and Paris were central for the Christian Middle Ages. The first impulses and principles of the Protestant Reformation emerged from Wittenberg's school of theology. The church opened its mind to the nineteenth century, thanks to Friedrich Schleiermacher's department of theology in Berlin. In American Christianity the seminaries have historically provided unique opportunities for involvement in both reflective disciplinary scholarship and practical Christian thinking that have shaped both the future of the church and society.

Two developments in recent decades need to be noted. Departments of religious studies are flourishing in secular colleges and universities. What is being taught "academically" in the theological schools, in terms of disciplines and subject matter, is being explored in these departments. The context and circumstances of teaching are different, but faculty for both are educated in the same graduate schools and are professionally influenced by one another. A primary form of this influence comes through the second development, the enhanced status of various national associations of religious scholars. The academic guild, such as the Society for Biblical Literature, the American Academy of Religion, and Society for Christian Ethics, determines standards, recognition, and status, and provides a network of communication within and between disciplines.[5]

Serving as the Intellectual Center of the Church

The third major missional purpose of a seminary is reflected in the classical vision of a theological school as an intellectual center of the church, seeking to increase the love of God and neighbor. In the middle of the twentieth century, theologian H. Richard Niebuhr claimed a dual function for the seminary: first as a place for the church to exercise its intellectual love of God and neighbor, and second, as a community bringing reflective criticism to bear on the church's worship, preaching, teaching, and care of souls.[6]

Not easily resolved is the tension in theological education between the "paideia" model of schooling for which knowledge of God and "forming persons' souls to be holy" remains foremost and the "professional" school model which stresses ministerial leadership and critical theological inquiry. David H. Kelsey has characterized these two polarities "Athens" and "Berlin," respectively, and suggests North American theological schools have always struggled with this dilemma.[7] H. Richard Niebuhr sought to capture both ends by emphasizing the "intellectual love of God and neighbor" as well as serving the Church through professional reflection and criticism of its worship, preaching, teaching, and the care of souls.[8] Few theological schools claim either the "Athens" or "Berlin" models exclusively. More common is some type of "compromise." For example, says Kelsey:

It may be an arrangement that factors out different aspects of the school's common life to the reign of each model of excellent schooling: the research university model may reign for faculty, . . . or for faculty in certain fields (say, church history, or biblical studies) but not in others (say, practical theology), while paideia reigns as the model for students, or only for students with a declared vocation to ordained ministry (so that other students aspiring to graduate school are free to attempt to meet standards set by the research university model); or research university values may be celebrated in relation to the school's official "academic" program, including both classroom expectations and the selection and rewarding of faculty, while the school's extracurricular life is shaped by commitments coming from the model provided paideia so that, for example, common worship is made central to their common life and a high premium is placed on the school being a residential community.[9]

Increasingly, however, as the twentieth century has been reaching a conclusion, the seminaries have become political battlegrounds for the churches, rather than intellectual centers open to the pursuit of truth. As various caucuses and interest groups within denominations have struggled for the soul of the church, they have targeted the takeover of seminaries as a high priority. President Neal F. Fisher of Garrett-Evangelical Theological Seminary has predicted that seminaries "can expect continuing and perhaps accelerating attempts to enlist the seminaries in the service of the agendas of both left and right."[10] Far from desiring reflective criticism being brought to bear on their theological principles or political practices, these caucuses seek moral justification of their causes and power to control the future of the seminaries.

Thus in a climate of political correctness, fostered by both right and left, the seminaries find it impossible to be noncombatants in the crossfire. Intellectual activity, even that promoted for the love of God and neighbor, gets absorbed in the struggle for the soul and structure of the church. Yet the integrity of the theological school demands it not be simply neutral in regard to great issues of justice or in the face of Machiavellian manipulation of the church. While it dare not become a blind partisan, it must speak the "truth in love" to all parties involved. Sometimes this may mean saying "no" to movements within the church that endanger the well-being of a seminary's intellectual attempt to love God and neighbor. Likewise it requires the seminary to be especially sensitive to the various voices within the church, lest it become indifferent to the variety of constituencies it seeks to serve.

These three fundamental purposes—preparation of preachers, education of the laity for ministry, and service as an intellectual center of the church—must be combined with two urgent priorities facing the contemporary church and seminary. Though the voices within the church are often at variance, they tend to unite on these priorities. In an era when Christian ministry often has been marginalized by society, and even sometimes by the church, it becomes imperative to underscore and upgrade this vital vocation.

Emphasizing God's Call for Ministry

Our first priority ought to be that of emphasizing God's call for ministry. Too often in the past we have emphasized ministry as a career, rather than as a sacred calling. True, it does provide a livelihood, but it is more than an occupation. Ministry is never a choice among professions, but a response to a summons from God. Whenever in the history of the church ministry has become more of a career than a calling, the mission of God has suffered and stagnated.[11]

Churches and seminaries are obligated to join together in asking persons if they have heard the call of Christ for ministry. The program of identification and enlistment of possible persons for professional service within the church should be high on our agendas, but this has not been the case for the last couple of decades, as we have at times seemed to have more people than positions to fill. Part of the problem, of course, has always been that of distribution—with God apparently calling more people to serve in sunny Florida than in the winters of Wyoming and more being led by the Spirit to suburban San Diego than to rural Last Chance, Colorado! Now as we see mounting evidence that there is a serious shortage in ministerial supply almost everywhere, it is of special importance that this dimension of our mutual partnership be once again underscored.

Crucial to the future of the church's mission and ministry are vital and vibrant theological schools preparing ordained and diaconal ministers who will effectively proclaim and live out the gospel of Jesus Christ. Recently I saw a photo of an empty pulpit with this haunting question beneath it: "Will anyone be preaching from the pulpit of your congregation in the year 2000?" The stark symbolism prompts reflection on what it will mean to many mainline Protestant denominations and Roman Catholicism if more persons are not prepared for ministry.

The decline in the number of persons preparing to be Catholic priests and nuns is well-known, but the myth of oversupply of Protestant clergy still persists in many quarters. A shortage gap between pulpit vacancies and graduating seminarians could have a profound impact on our churches, large and small, urban and rural. Increasingly we will face the temptation to post "Out of Business" signs on our smaller churches, or we will utilize persons for our parishes who may be neither well-prepared nor steeped in the ethos and values of our denominations.

Increasingly, seminaries are seeking to be at the forefront of efforts to lift the call of Christ to ministry. For many years a "surplus" mentality permeated Protestant churches, and efforts to recruit the brightest and most promising for Christ's ministry were neglected. Yet clearly if supply is to meet future demand, we must have more persons responding positively to God's call and preparing themselves to serve parishes.

In seeking out future pastors and diaconal ministers for Christ's church, we need to remember that ministry is not just a matter of gifts and evidence of God's grace; it also has to do with faith and the fruits of faith. All four dimensions were stressed by John Wesley, but we have often reduced the requirements simply to gifts and graces, as if talents and personality are all that is required. Evangelicals, in particular, have retained an emphasis on belief and disciplined discipleship that is essential to ministry. Seminaries, however, cannot produce effective ministers from persons who lack even the minimal gifts and graces needed. Curriculums cannot fully address subtleties of character. Preaching courses can refine talent but cannot create silver-tongued orators from lead minds and iron hearts. Personal qualities like imagination, creativity, empathy, stability, spiritual depth, humility, and sensibility are not only hard to measure and report, but even more impossible to teach. Persons should not be encouraged to enroll in our seminaries if they don't have at least latent qualities and abilities that will enrich the future leadership of the church. Mediocrity in ministry is a curse upon the church and society.

Thus, one of our greatest needs is a new partnership of church and seminary that will emphasize Christ's call for ministry, helping to identify the brightest and most promising persons for ministry and enrollment in our schools. With the prospect of at least 40 percent of our ordained pastors in some mainline denominations retiring at the age of 65 by the year 2000 (and all indications are that this percentage will probably be much higher), then we must begin *now* if we are to truly serve the church and world.

The Most Overpaid Profession in the World

Our second priority ought to be underscoring the supreme value and importance of the ministerial calling and vocation. More than thirty years ago, I learned from Bob and Polly Holmes that the Christian ministry is "the most overpaid profession in the world." In a small pamphlet, they introduced me to a startling discovery of the deeper meanings and values of a life vocation committed to Christ.

Can we imagine anything more contradictory or incongruous than claiming ministry as the most overpaid profession in the world? A quick review of statistics should demolish easily such simplistic thinking. For unless you happen to become a bishop, a seminary president, or a "big steeple" pulpiteer, the chances of having a high salary in the ministry are indeed slim. Entering the ordained or diaconal ministry because you expect to join the ranks of highly paid professionals such as medical doctors and lawyers is to likely invite yourself to a lifetime of disappointment and disillusionment. To accept God's calling in Christ for ministry is to open oneself to a life, if not of economic insecurity, then of at least living from paycheck to paycheck.

Yes, a convincing case can be made that the clergy are not the most overpaid profession in the world, but let us not be too comfortable in dismissing the deeper truth to which Bob and Polly Holmes were pointing. Probing deeper their paradoxical phrase that the Christian ministry is "the most overpaid profession in the world," they remind us anew of the deeper meanings and values of a life vocation. Economic statistics may dispute the assertion that clergy are an overpaid profession, but on another level I sense a profound truth that many a minister can authenticate. Resonant within my soul rings a bell reminding me of why I have been called to be a minister of the gospel of Jesus Christ.

The opening thoughts of their pamphlet echo in my heart today just as much as the first time I read them. A person isn't involved in ministry very long before he or she "discovers that there's more drama" in hospital rooms and airplane terminals than in all paperback novels, and "more real-life adventure in homes of ordinary people than on the TV screens in all their living rooms." Persons in ministry never die from boredom or lack of excitement. Ministers are in touch with "the most important happenings of people's lives" and "on the inside of the deepest struggles in their experiences."[12]

In poetic and powerful language Bob and Polly Holmes sketch a portrait of a pastor in comparison and relationship with other professions. They celebrate both the joy and challenges of ministry, writing:

> I'm not a physician, but I've stood at many a bedside when a life hung in the balance. I'm not an attorney, but I've sat in court through many an anxious trial. I'm not a law-enforcement officer, and yet I have been on the scene—all the way from barroom to jail, from second-floor flat to state reform school, reaching for people who need desperately to be reached and understood and helped. I'm not a judge nor an FBI agent nor a psychiatrist, and yet my job is to try to bring justice to bear on injustice, truth on falsehood, and love on hate.

Sometimes pastors say they still can't believe they get paid for doing what they love doing. Far from feeling underpaid, many would gladly serve without compensation. Most would say that "in actuality, no one gets paid like a pastor—in satisfaction for doing the Lord's work, in the opportunity to draw close to God while 'at work,' and in relationships with some of God's most wonderful saints."[13]

The freedom of ministry cannot really be measured by any price index. In a single day, a clergyperson, unlike any other professional, may have the liberty of praying with a patient just before surgery, counseling a troubled teenager, demonstrating in a protest march, preaching a funeral service, and raising funds for global mission projects. And so the litany of life and the music of ministry goes. Speaking of ministry:

> Underpaid? Not my profession! The fact that in this job you are dealing with people as they really are, facing their real needs and finding the real solution to their problems, is payment enough. In watching a troubled person face himself or herself for the first time, hearing them break out in their first real, honest soul-searching confession—seeing them reach out for their first grasp for help outside of themselves—you are watching a Gracious God at work. You are glimpsing all the possibilities that have lain dormant in a human soul, waiting for someone to bring that soul into the circuit so that God's power can flow into it and make it live again. What greater privilege could any human occupation hold?
>
> In the life-work I have undertaken, I have received more confidence than I had ever thought possible, more meaning and purpose than I had ever dreamed of, far more satisfaction than I have ever deserved. Therefore, I affirm without qualification that the Christian ministry is the most overpaid profession in the world.[14]

Yes, this vision of ministry as the most overpaid profession in the world has grasped my soul and claimed my life for more than thirty years. More and more persons today are anxious to hear this paradoxical message anew and to respond to God's call for ministry. It is time for the church and seminary to proclaim it loudly once again as we prepare for mission in the twenty-first century. Economic statistics may not verify that the ministry of the Good Shepherd ranks as the most overpaid profession in the world, but no other calling can quite match it! "How beautiful" indeed will be "the feet of those who bring good news" along the city streets, rural roads, parish paths, hospital hallways, prison corridors, and the emerging new information superhighway of the future.

CHAPTER TWO

A New Assault on the Seminaries

We must no longer be children, tossed to and fro and blown about by every wind of doctrine, by people's trickery, by their craftiness in deceitful scheming. But speaking the truth in love, we must grow up in every way into him who is the head, into Christ.

EPHESIANS 4:14-15

B laming the seminaries for the weaknesses of the clergy or the church has long been a popular sport in certain ecclesiastical circles. What is good and positive is assumed to happen despite formal theological education, while what is less than desirable is attributed to what is wrong with our seminaries.

In the turmoil of contemporary life, as churches struggle to maintain identity and membership, the seminaries, be they Roman Catholic or Protestant (evangelical or mainstream) are often caught in the whirlwind of conflict and controversy engulfing denominations. Sometimes they serve as convenient scapegoats for all that seems to have gone awry in the church. What good they do seems to be minimized, while the faults of the seminaries are maximized.

The Myth of the Perfect Seminary

Public criticisms of theological education certainly are not new. Beware of perpetuating the myth that once the perfect seminary or ministry existed. The "old song" of pastoral declension or deterioration has been sung about preachers ever since the second generation of New England pastors emerged.[1]

As early as 1924 a critical study of ministerial formation "grew out of the widely held belief that the machinery and the methods used in educating Protestant ministers were inadequate. It was asserted that the number and the quality of ministerial candidates had been on the decline for some time and that churches faced a crisis because of the real or the prospective dearth of leaders."[2] In 1938 many reports received from different parts of the world, "stated that there are ministers of a poor standard of education, who are unable to win the respect of the laity and to lead the churches, that some are out of touch with the realities of life and the needs of their people, and are not distinguished by zeal for Christian service in the community."[3] In 1956 it was alleged that "the theological schools of the churches in America share all the perplexities of the contemporary Protestant Community and its ministry . . . the first impression they give is . . . an impression of uncertainty of purpose."[4] Change, not decline, best describes seminaries and pastors over the years.

An Orchestrated Chorus of Critics

In recent years a new assault on the seminaries has been launched, not by secular or anti-Christian forces, but by internal political critics, suffering from deep dissatisfaction with the theological temperature of the schools and/or attempting to gain political control in a particular denomination. This attack has taken various forms depending on the denomination and context. The Vatican has exerted pressure on its seminaries and censored its theologians in an effort to limit their openness to experimentation and creative theological thought. Southern Baptists have captured the headlines with their massive battles between "moderates" and "conservatives" to control the boards of their denominations, often resulting in dramatic "firings" of seminary presidents and faculty replacements. Political caucuses within mainline Protestant denominations have engaged in ceaseless sniper fire and guerrilla warfare aimed at destroying the credibility of their seminaries and weakening their financial support, hoping thereby to wrest control and direction of their theological schools.

Representative of this new assault on the seminaries is the recent book *Requiem: A Lament in Three Movements,* penned by Drew University theology professor Thomas C. Oden. His book blitz was preceded by a series of high profile speeches and publications sponsored by the more conservative political edge of The United Methodist Church.[5] After a distinguished teaching and publishing career,[6] Oden has repented of his past liberal and even radical socialistic perspectives, and wholeheartedly has embraced an "orthodox evangelical" position.[7] With the fervor of a new convert, he tends to justify his new stance by distorting and demeaning that which he has rejected.

If it were true, Oden's portrait of the contemporary seminary indeed would prove frightening to the average "middle American" churchgoer. In his imaginative projection of the typical seminary, students are engaged in endless sexual experimentation and faced with a faculty dominated by ultrafeminist neo-pagans, extreme relativists, permissive moralists, and quasi-Marxist liberators. More conservative, evangelical students are harassed from day one about their beliefs, lifestyles, and even the hymns they prefer to sing. Heresies abound. Homosexuality reigns. Historical amnesia prevails. And faculty live and work without a care for the welfare and future of the local congregation.

In contrast, this book paints a different picture of what is happening at our seminaries today, not ignoring their faults and problems, but focusing instead on genuine, not distorted, dilemmas and challenges. In language hopefully less acidic or acerbic and therefore probably less colorful, I have attempted to interpret a vision of theological education appropriate for mission and ministry in the twenty-first century, yet faithful to the biblical and theological mandates of historic Christianity.[8]

Stimulated by Oden's recent criticisms, I have sought in this book to examine the issues he passionately sets forth, as well as other dilemmas facing theological education today. Oden is not a soloist singing *a cappella,* but part of an orchestrated chorus of critics, from both right and left, who seek to reform, if not revolutionize, theological education. Paul Wilkes in *The Atlantic Monthly* early in the 1990s painted a critical portrait of America's Protestant, Catholic, and Jewish seminaries in his article "The Hands That

Would Shape Our Souls." Timothy C. Morgan's account in *Christianity Today* of "Re-engineering the Seminary," qualifies as a thoughtful evangelical example, while from the more liberal left comes the feminist challenge called *God's Fierce Whimsy,* edited by Katie G. Cannon and others.[9]

Renewed Vitality for the Church's Mission and Ministry

While Oden's speeches and book provide a stimulus or spur for this reflective assessment and theological articulation, my primary motivation for writing flows from a deep commitment to the renewed vitality of the church's mission and ministry and an appreciation of the role the seminaries have and can play in this revitalization process. I do not attempt a point by point rebuttal of Oden's diatribe, but instead invite laity and clergy into dialogue about the critical questions and issues that face both the church and theological education as we move into the next millennium.[10] Certainly reform is required, but let us enter intelligently and prayerfully into discussion, lest we destroy individuals and institutions who have faithfully sought to serve the cause of Jesus Christ over the years.

Illustrative is the dilemma facing The Theological School of Drew University. Since one of its own professors has chosen to launch an attack against mainstream theological schools by highlighting one incident on the Drew campus and generally not naming any other schools or persons (an exception being Episcopal Divinity School of Cambridge, Massachusetts), the tendency is to believe he is writing from his Drew experience. Though he claims he is not attacking his own institution, he certainly has run the risk of damaging the reputation of his seminary and his colleagues.[11] Drew, with its incredible history of excellence in theological education, deserves better. When Drew's faculty or administration now attempts to set the record straight, they appear to be defensive. Instead they deserve an apology, for few seminaries in this nation can match Drew's outstanding contribution to the mission and ministry of the church around the world.

Unloving Critics and Critical Lovers

The message in the book of Ephesians (4:14-15) remains essential to the well-being of both the contemporary church and seminary. Neither should be "tossed to and fro and blown about by every wind of doctrine, by people's trickery, by their craftiness in deceitful scheming." By "speaking the truth in love" to one another, both church and seminary have the potential of growing "up in every way into him who is the head, into Christ."

The challenge is how to avoid the extremes. Uncritical lovers of either church or seminary simply bless the status quo, refusing to acknowledge areas of weakness or corruption. Unloving critics blindly and callously unleash unfair and often vitriolic attacks. Critical lovers, on the other hand, express a deep and abiding affection for the other, but feel obligated to speak "the truth in love" by sharing genuine criticisms in the hope that the beloved can be enhanced and improved.

An educational product and tenured beneficiary of contemporary theological education himself, Oden's own self-description of previously championing the current system for the past three decades indicates he was somewhat of an uncritical lover. Since now his comments at points have become vitriolic and his arguments hyperbolic, the temptation persists to classify him as an unloving critic with his own personal agenda and theological ax to grind. But that would be to dismiss him too easily. Like a loving critic, his professed motivation is not to destroy and injure the church and theological education, or even to enhance his own reputation and fame in evangelical circles, but to rescue and restore his beloved church and seminaries.

Having served as a church-related college and seminary president for almost twenty-five years, I have long struggled with the inherent tensions between church and its higher education institutions. While I take strong exception especially to the tone of Oden's presentations, I welcome his invitation to explore the truth of his perceptions and perspectives.

Mean-spirited "trashing" of other people's positions too often permeates both academia and the church. Instead of fruitful critiques, persons descend into dismissive approaches, misrepresenting arguments, distorting evidence, and maligning motives. Cornel West, perhaps America's foremost African American intellectual, warns against such "trashing," which not only serves to fan and fuel an immobilizing polarization, but also obscures the basic issues at stake. Instead West contends "we must try to present the most subtle and sympathetic interpretation of an opponent's viewpoints." Truly "vigorous criticism rises above the level of trashing when it locates and appreciates both insights and blindnesses, tensions and inconsistencies within the view of a worthy opponent."[12]

In that reconciling spirit, commensurate with the scriptural mandate in Ephesians to "speak the truth in love," I hope to set forth not simply responses to criticisms (such as Oden's) but a vision of theological education appropriate "for the better preparation and education of persons called to the high and holy office of the Christian ministry" in the twenty-first century.

The lessons to be learned from this debate, I trust, transcend the United Methodist arena in which they are being fought. Readers are invited to look beyond the particular and peculiar United Methodist illustrations to their own denominational and ecumenical contexts. Tensions exist between churches and seminaries of all denominations. Political forces of various types seek to capture dissension and use it for their own purposes. The freedom of theological inquiry and the integrity of our seminary institutions remain ever threatened by ideological captivity.

Six Major Criticisms of Contemporary Seminaries

Yale theologian David H. Kelsey, in a recent book about theological schools called *To Understand God Truly,* notes that "grumbling" or to "complain vigorously" typically characterizes American seminaries. Based on his studious observation of theological schools across the country, he contends criticism varies depending on one's role and status in relation to the school. The quest for perfection never ceases.

Endless student complaints about the curriculum range from assertions that it is excessively "academic" and "theoretical" to insufficiently "professional" and "practical" to not adequately "integrated" to so dominated by the "professional ministers" model as not to allow for individual intellectual interests. Other complaints focus on the insufficient "pluralism" of the student body and faculty, with limited numbers of women and persons of color. Faculty have their own set of grievances. These include concerns about excessive teaching loads that prohibit research and publication. Some express fear that church expectations for their leadership and participation deny them time for keeping up with the literature in their fields. Others express dissatisfaction with seminary policies and benefits, lack of library resources, inability to influence governance, and so on. Administrators and trustees worry about the above, plus questions of financing, student recruitment, and personnel problems.[13]

Selecting six major criticisms proves almost impossible when one recognizes the self-critical nature of the seminary community. For purposes of this discussion, therefore, I have chosen to address those criticisms most recently leveled against mainline Protestant theological education in the previously mentioned book and articles by Thomas C. Oden. In my judgment, these six are not necessarily the most serious or perplexing, but since they have received the most church press and conference assembly attention, they deserve special consideration. The alienation reflected in these charges must be of major concern since they are coming from valued church constituencies of the mainline denominational seminaries.

First, contemporary seminaries are criticized for self-cloning look-alike faculties.[14] Since the primary responsibility for recommending new professors rests with established faculty, particularly those with expertise in a particular discipline, the possibility of perpetuating clones always threatens. Evangelical concern is heightened if current faculties match one description portrayed by Oden: "doctrinally imaginative, liturgically experimental, disciplinarily nonjudgmental, politically correct, multiculturally tolerant, morally broad-minded, ethically situationist, and, above all, sexually lenient, permissive, uninhibited."[15] Another of his portraits suggests white males are pariahs[16] and that faculty candidates are preferred "who have not been contaminated by any exposure to local church practice or any strong tradition of piety."[17] Especially criticized is the

39

presence of persons on the faculty who are characterized as being ultrafeminist, plus the absence and oppression of evangelicals or "traditionalists."[18]

Far from being self-cloned and look-alike, seminary faculties today look significantly different from when I was a student some thirty years ago at Boston University and Harvard Divinity School. Indeed, in six years of master's and doctoral work, I studied under only one white woman and one African American male scholar. Thank God, faculties have not continued to be self-cloning as they were in a previous age, and more opportunities now exist for women and persons of color to hold tenured teaching positions, once the exclusive prerogative of white males. Today's limited diversity hardly justifies claims that we white men are disappearing from the seminary scene! The latest report of the Association of Theological Schools reports that 71.9 percent of all faculty in our seminaries are white males and 17.5 percent are white females. Persons of color comprise only 10.6 percent (8.4 percent male and 2.2 percent female).[19] Faculty sexual orientation is not reported, but professors who are openly gay and lesbian are no doubt statistically small.

Finding faculty with extended parish experience, who are also current with the scholarship in their disciplines, is truly a dilemma. Neither Oden with his thirty-five years of tenured teaching nor I with my twenty-five years in administration are exactly models to be emulated! What is often overlooked in discussions centering on this problem is that, with rare exception, seminary faculty are active in their own local congregations as well as in regional and national activities of their denomination. Such lay and clergy experience, while not equivalent to serving as a parish pastor, should not be totally discounted. Bias merely against having parish experience or being pious, of course, would be inexcusable, but Oden provides no illustrations to buttress his claims of prejudice. President Lovett H. Weems, Jr. reports that at The Saint Paul School of Theology all the faculty "are actively involved in the church, and our seventeen faculty have had a total of 161 years of full-time ministry."[20]

Earlier in the twentieth century, a particular brand of theology (such as neoorthodoxy, personalism, process thought, and so on) dominated a faculty and curriculum. Currently, however, greater diversity exists, with faculty deliberately seeking to include perspectives different from their own. If evangelical or "traditionalist" perspectives are missing, then conservative students need to insist on their inclusion, just as women and persons of color must constantly press for greater awareness of their experiences and theological representatives. Likewise, historically evangelical schools will want to review their curriculum offerings and faculties to see if they have included more liberal theological perspectives. The norms of excellence demand no less.

A corrective to the possibilities of a self-cloning faculty is the role of administrations and governance boards. Oden, who has operated from a university-based faculty system, fails to mention the varieties of faculty selection in freestanding seminaries, where administrators and trustees play an important role in selection and approval of faculties. No one system prevails. Deans and presidents often have veto powers. Some mainline seminaries have trustees on search committees; others would require votes by their boards on issues of appointment; probably all require trustee approval for rank and tenure decisions. Some denominations even require endorsement of faculty, beyond that given by a local board. All systems have imperfections, but checks and balances do exist to guard against inappropriate faculty appointments and to ensure quality in theological teaching.

Second, theological schools are accused of being tradition-deprived.[21] Contemporary seminaries have been described as suffering from amnesia, as being "tradition-impaired," forgetting or ignoring much of Christianity's past. Of particular concern to Oden is the tendency to ignore or downgrade the teaching of church fathers like Athanasius, Augustine, and Thomas Aquinas. He describes his own theological preference as being "postmodern paleo-orthodoxy,"[22] with an emphasis on the theological writings of the first five centuries. He contends that the doctrines of incarnation and resurrection are dismissed.[23] He portrays evangelicals as having to struggle to get the equal right to be heard along "with social activists, new age nativists, ultrafeminists, Gaia (breathing earth) theorists, animal rights advocates, champions of oral and anal sex with either or both genders, and radical speculative biblical critics."[24] Evangelicals are guilty of "a chronic case of amnesia concerning the saints and martyrs and consensual writers of the earliest Christian centuries, preferring to leap from the present back to Scripture over centuries of exegesis, without the intrusion of the great minds of the church."[25] He cites seven seminaries in particular that are not tradition-impaired: St. Vladimir's (Orthodox Church in America), Duke (United Methodist), Trinity Episcopal School for Ministry, St. Charles Borromeo (Roman Catholic) in Philadelphia, St. Mary's (Roman Catholic) in Maryland, Wycliffe Hall (Anglican) at Oxford, and Regents (Interdenominational) in Vancouver, Canada.[26]

This vision of seminaries without an appreciation of history and with such distorted curriculums must seem strange and horrifying to those not personally involved in seminary study. It is hard to imagine curriculums dominated by animal rights advocates, new age nativists, and faculty suffering from historical amnesia. *The reason it is hard to imagine is because it is simply not true. It is fiction, not fact.*

I do not know what evidence exists to justify claims that the doctrines of incarnation and resurrection are being denied or discounted. Throughout Christian history theologians have sought to interpret these beliefs in their contexts and times. In listening to seminary sermons and reading manuscripts written by seminary faculty I hear and see similar efforts underway currently. I don't doubt that a few scattered faculty may disavow these two doctrines, but I am deeply puzzled as to why seminaries as a whole should be smeared as being unfriendly to evangelical students in these matters of faith.

Examine any seminary catalog and you will discover the curriculum is deeply steeped in historical studies. Students are required to understand the 2000 years of Christian history. It is quite impossible to study the Bible, theology, or practically any other discipline without being submerged into deep historical waters. For more than a decade, outsiders (such as persons from retirement homes, active pastors, visiting district superintendents, prospective students, and so on) at The Iliff School of Theology, for example, have been sitting in on classes. Never once have I heard that the curriculum was devoid of tradition and dominated by pop culture. I suspect similar testimony could be heard at Luther

Northwestern Theological Seminary, Fuller Theological Seminary, Perkins School of Theology of Southern Methodist University, Princeton Theological Seminary, Interdenominational Theological Center, Wesley Theological Seminary, and hundreds of others. In every one of these distinguished places of theological learning, I expect they could both denounce and demonstrate that the following assertion by Oden is simply untrue and unfair:

> In the last decade the curriculum of seminaries has been liberated for sexually permissive advocacy, political activism, and ultrafeminist hype (as distinguished from believing feminist argument). The study of Bible and church history becomes a deconstruction of patriarchal texts and traditions. The study of ethics becomes the study of political correctness. The study of liturgy becomes an experiment in color, balloons, poetry, and freedom. The study of pastoral care becomes a support group for the sexually alienated.[27]

Authentic criticism needs to be directed at the seminaries, but this needs to be tempered by the ninth commandment: "Thou shalt not bear false witness against thy neighbour" (Exodus 20:16).

Third, "the tenure principle, which was designed to protect academic freedom, has become so exploited as now to protect academic license, absenteeism, incompetence, and at times moral turpitude." [28] Oden portrays a "point of no return" when almost all teaching slots are occupied by tenured radicals "who have little in common with the institution's historic mission or the constituency's values or the church's tradition."[29] Combine this concern with his description of faculty "organizing for perks, plums, and pay" and fears of tenured faculty escalate.[30] This is particularly true when "a controlling ethic of personal, hedonistic, individual self-actualization pervades the immutably tenured professor's choices about what to teach in elective courses. The selection of course topics may focus more on the professor's personal fulfillment and private interests than on curricular needs."[31]

For good reason, tenure has always had its critics. The danger constantly exists that mediocrity will be rewarded and protected. Once some professors receive tenure, they may tend to be less diligent in their scholarship or teaching responsibilities. The abuse of tenure does happen, but the total experience of universities and seminaries over the years has been that the limited cases of misuse are not comparable to the great benefits derived from having a faculty with sufficient security to be free to explore wherever the search for truth leads them.

Once again Oden's imagination runs ahead of his data, and he provides not a single example of tenured faculty guilty of academic license, absenteeism, incompetence, or moral turpitude. Academic Dean Glenn T. Miller of Bangor Theological Seminary declares that as a fellow evangelical he doesn't think Oden provides "a sound or accurate analysis of present-day theological education." For example, Oden fails to give names. "If heresy and scholarly irresponsibility exist, they must be incarnated someplace and somewhere," says Miller. "If this type of corruption exists, tell us who, when, and where."[32]

Oden also fails to mention that all tenure policies have methods for dealing with precisely these problems should they arise. His own proposal is to replace tenure with something called "continuing status." Amazingly, he would leave the powers of decision with the faculty, so his idea is hardly revolutionary.[33] Seminaries already have detailed procedures by which persons are evaluated yearly before being granted tenure. Freestanding seminaries involve their trustees in these deliberations to safeguard against the types of abuse Oden envisions. Likewise, after tenure is granted, various reviews continue which are used to evaluate and improve teaching and research, determine promotions, and set salary scales. University-related divinity schools must defend their appointments and tenure decisions in a rigorous review process that includes upper levels of university administration, trustees, and sometimes, review by outside experts.

The image of tenured faculty functioning without supervision, and following just the dictates of their own wishes without regard to institutional and curriculum needs, is a possibility, but hardly a probability in the vast majority of struggling seminaries in this land. Neal F. Fisher says Oden's intemperate condemnation doesn't fit the overwhelming majority of faculty members. They "began their ministry as a Christian calling and continue to labor with devotion, as one professor expressed to me, 'to help a new generation of pastors to love the Scriptures and teach and preach them faithfully.' "[34]

Fourth, academic freedom in the seminaries has become an excuse for dodging criticism from the churches.[35] Thomas C. Oden claims that seminaries avoid "dialogue with church constituencies by claiming that professors have the freedom to teach anything they please under the flag of ordinal preparation. If the liberated have the freedom to teach apostasy, the believing church has the freedom to withhold its consent. If they teach countercanonical doctrines and conjectures inimical to the health of the church, the church has no indelible moral obligation to give them support or to bless their follies."[36] Speaking specifically, he suggests that Reformed and Wesleyan traditions (namely the Westminster Confession and Twenty-five Articles of Faith) are no longer implemented.[37]

The principle of academic freedom has been endorsed by quality institutions of higher education in order to protect the pursuit of truth from the manipulations of administrators, the pressure of interest groups, and the temptation to avoid honesty in order to conform to standards of popular appeal. Some denominational traditions, such as United Methodism, have long histories of defending academic freedom, believing excellence in education is best preserved in this manner. Like tenure, this principle runs the risk of abuse in the short run, but in the long term it has proven to be invaluable in resisting the shifting winds of ecclesiastical and doctrinal trends.

Far from resisting dialogue with church constituencies, every seminary supported by the church that I know anything about is in constant conversation with church agencies and congregations. Oden says that "funding sources for seminary education are belatedly learning to insist on accountability to grassroots constituencies."[38] Having spent the past twenty-five years engaged in "grassroots" fund-raising, I personally see nothing "belated" about this idea. Perhaps Oden has lived in a university world that didn't require this type of accountability, but the rest of us have been working hard at dialogue, interpretation, and fund-raising.

For funding purposes United Methodist seminaries must annually submit extensive reports to the General Board of Higher Education and Ministry. A Commission on Theological Education for the denomination continuously reviews the school's standards. Another denominational committee advises and approves the standards for teaching United Methodist history, doctrine, and polity. The University Senate once every ten years determines whether the seminary qualifies to be listed as a United Methodist seminary. Fund-raising requires administrators and faculty to be in constant dialogue with church constituencies. Regular correspondence and conversation is carried on with conference Boards of Ministry, both ordained and diaconal. Additionally, the thirteen officially related United Methodist seminaries have launched a major national project, called Agenda 21, which involves faculty and administrative dialogue with laity and clergy. These continuous conversations assure that United Methodist seminaries can never be isolated from the church's loving criticism as well as, thankfully, its critical engagement and support.

Fifth, theological schools recognize no theological or ethical boundaries. This has created a condition that never before has existed in Christian history—the nonexistence of heresy.[39] The lack of theological integrity and discipline has resulted in theological teaching that has nothing to do with God, revelation, the church, or worship. Oden says theology in the seminaries can now include:

> anything from alpha rhythms to Zen, from comparative anthropology to socialist dialectics, from semiotics to sand castles, from gender research to flower arrangement, from chaos theory to cholesterol control. There is no assumed requirement that "theo"logy thus conceived need have anything whatever to do with the revealed God. It can be poetry or astrology or parapsychology, and maybe by next year it will be weather forecasting or oral hygiene.[40]

No doubt there has been a misuse of the term theology in certain quarters, but Oden provides a deliberately distorted caricature of what his seminary colleagues in theology teach.

Sometimes in reading his book, I think Oden thinks of himself as the Rush Limbaugh of theology, employing sarcastic humor to buttress his points.[41] The problem is that he is not funny, but bizarre when he bends the truth and makes it sound like the seminaries are using God's name "to mean little more than weight loss, dream analysis, exotic vitamins, salesmanship, yoga, LSD, and psychodrama."[42] If it were true, who would disagree? Yet he produces not a shred of evidence to justify his claims. His greatest complaints theologically focus around the subject of "Sophia," and the two instances he cites don't directly involve seminary faculty. The "Sophia worship" he alleges happened in the Drew University chapel was led by a visiting pastor, not a Drew faculty member.

Oden's credibility about these matters has been called into question. His allegations about what happened at Drew have been sharply questioned by the Drew Theological Alumni/ae Association. In a letter mailed to all Drew graduates, it is reported that no other Drew faculty member who attended the particular worship experience agrees with his understanding and interpretation of what happened! Further, the president of the association declares that after thorough investigation:

> Be assured that there was *no* goddess worship in Craig Chapel. Faculty members who attended the service pointed out that the words of Institution were from the United Methodist Book of Worship. The invitation to the Table was given in the name of Jesus Christ and not given in the name of Sophia as reported in an article by faculty member Thomas Oden. While there were references to wisdom in the liturgy of the service, all of them were from the Bible.[43]

As for Oden's obsession with heresy, his professorial colleague in theology at Drew University Theological School, Catherine Keller, reminds Oden and us that "apostasy" and "heresy" are quite un-Methodist terms. Lest we suffer from historical amnesia, she wrote in *The Christian Century:*

> Charging "apostasy," pronouncing "heresy," demanding purges—what sort of language is this for Methodism, whose founders, concerned more with warming the heart than with freezing the doctrine, were themselves accused of femininity and heresy? And for Christianity? The rhetoric of heresy and purge has nothing at all to do with the language of the biblical Jesus, the one who was a victim, never a perpetrator, of heresy hunting.[44]

Almost one hundred years ago, at the turn of the century, the various predecessors of The United Methodist Church were engaged in heresy trials involving Borden Parker Bowne, Hinckley G. Mitchell, and Phillip Schaff. As a result of these ideological struggles, in 1912 the church declared that no longer would bishops of the Methodist Church be responsible for approving all faculty appointments. An open environment of academic freedom for the seminaries was determined. As F. Thomas Trotter, former President of Alaska Pacific University, has noted, "a striking fact is that the schools remain free of intrusion by the denomination in their curricula, administration, and vision for the church. This ambience of care and support on the part of the denomination and the sensitivity and respect on the part of the seminaries is one of the great gifts of church life in our time."[45]

Criticism to be fair must be carefully done and accurately researched. When seminaries or faculty stray from appropriate boundaries of truth and falsehood, right and wrong, then they need to be challenged. A case in point currently is an emphasis on increasing awareness of the potential for, and ending, sexual misconduct and eliminating sexual harassment in our churches and seminaries.

Oden might have done the church and seminaries a favor by thoughtful criticism, but instead he has embarked on an ideological crusade. Why, for example, in his book does he dwell on the incident in the Drew Chapel, using it to illustrate the excesses of mainstream seminaries, and then in a closing remark in the obscure appendix to the book say: "I think the vitality of our chapel life is better now than in most times of my thirty-five years of teaching in seminaries."[46] He goes on to say he wasn't attacking seminary or faculty leadership. He even acknowledges that "it happened only once here, and I doubt it will happen again. I have no interest in fanning the flames of controversy or eliciting hysterical responses to eccentric events."[47] If he truthfully was not interested in "fanning the flames of controversy" why has he repeatedly written and spoken about this event in contexts hostile to his and other mainline seminaries? There is something ultimately tragic about Oden. Why does he wait until the appendix of his book to declare "Sophia worship is so patently out of the mainstream of consensual ecumenical liturgy that I have little fear that it is suddenly about to take over our seminaries"?[48] Why leave such a truthful statement to the obscure end, while exploiting the sensationalism at the beginning? What theological and ethical boundaries does he observe?

Sixth, a disdain for evangelicals is everywhere evident in mainstream seminaries.[49] Some evangelicals view themselves as the most marginalized and oppressed group, particularly in regard to faculty appointments. Oden even has the audacity to compare them with Jews during the Holocaust who were forced to wear the Star of David on their clothes. Prospective evangelical seminarians are warned they may receive bad grades because of their theology or because they love the hymns of Fanny Crosby.[50] "No heresy of any kind any longer exists," says Oden, except "offenses against inclusivism."[51] Thus, instead of unconditional love and acceptance, they should anticipate being "excluded or ostracized" because of "gender, social location, political values, sexual ethics, or doctrinal orthodoxy."[52] Evangelical students even should be prepared to face intimidation and professors may be "ambushed in entrapment situations by ultrafeminists."[53] Yet Oden urges evangelical and orthodox students to attend mainline seminaries, since they may constitute the "only viable hope for transforming tradition-impaired seminaries."[54]

What bothers Oden about the rhetoric of inclusiveness troubles many others in theological education: namely, that true inclusiveness sometimes does not exist, as nonliberals are willfully excluded.[55] Oden correctly identifies the temptation of liberals to give lip service to inclusiveness yet find various reasons to exclude more conservative voices from the theological marketplace of ideas. Even while writing this book, I was challenged for having invited Robert H. Schuller from the Crystal Cathedral to speak at The Iliff Week of Graduate Lectures and Rocky Mountain Pastors' School. I even had to answer threats that the "freedom of the pulpit" should be denied him in Denver, even though he has an estimated weekly audience of 20 million viewers via 184 countries on all seven continents. The irony was that those who opposed Schuller did not advocate canceling the next night's speaker, Episcopal Bishop John Spong, whose views favoring the ordination of gays and lesbians are quite contrary to stated policies of The United Methodist Church. The integrity and vitality of churches and seminaries makes the defense of both freedom of the pulpit and academic freedom indispensable in the search for truth and justice. With Carl Sandburg I agree that the ugliest word in the English language is exclusiveness.

Claiming a victim status, however, equivalent to persons of color, women, or even Jews murdered in the Holocaust is hardly becoming or appropriate of evangelicals.[56] The presence and power of evangelicals in the church and seminary remains far more substantial than those who have been systematically excluded over the years. Liberal and evangelical white Christians (especially males) cannot so easily escape responsibility for historic and contemporary racism and sexism by now pleading victimization.

While it is not possible to verify Oden's claim that one-third of all seminarians are evangelicals or pietists, the number certainly may be correct. It could be even greater. Their presence in any theological school adds to the richness of the religious experience and ought to be mutually beneficial. They need to be challenged by the intellectual resources of the schools. Their deep convictions and disciplined lifestyle make them potentially excellent candidates for the ministry. All seminaries should be most hospitable to their presence and participation. Every effort should be made to welcome their involvement, learn from their faith, and encourage their spiritual journey. If they are treated as nonpersons, this is a serious violation of the gospel and seminary faculty and communities must make reparations.

Again Oden exaggerates to make his point. Instances of downgrading because of orthodox Christian views need to be documented. Every seminary has an appeal process for mistreatment. Outsiders always need to be aware that complaints may have no substance. A year ago I heard rumors that students at my seminary were not being treated fairly in terms of financial aid. When I checked, I was shocked to discover that no one had even filed a complaint or grievance about financial aid for four years, much less was there any grounds for the grumbling. As to getting lower grades for singing Fanny Crosby's hymns, that is even more unlikely. Not every faculty member may love her hymns, but the vast majority would join me in singing songs from *The United Methodist Hymnal* (which Oden also condemns as being "politically correct"[57]) like "To God Be the Glory," "Jesus, Keep Me Near the Cross," "Pass Me Not, O Gentle Savior," "Blessed Assurance," "I Am Thine, O Lord," and "Rescue the Perishing."

Repentance and a New Partnership of Church and Seminary

In responding to these and other criticisms, it is abundantly clear that past relationships between church and seminary have not always been ideal. All parties involved have at times been arrogant and unjust. Truly, as theologian Charles M. Wood has noted "there is a place for repentance in the life of the theological school."[58] We in the seminary community must acknowledge and apologize for our sins and shortcomings in failing to be truly the servants of the church. Too often our academic concerns have taken priority over our church commitments. Likewise, the church needs to reassess its relationship and attitude at points. Repentance and a new partnership between church and seminary appears imperative.

Certain images come to mind when I think of our past relationships. You could easily add others. "Playing the blaming game," for example, has often led the church to accuse the seminary of failing to prepare students by not requiring the right courses or being too theoretical. The seminaries have countered by noting the poor quality of students produced by the church, claiming we "can't make silk purses out of sows' ears."

A second image or relationship we often invoke is that of "Glorious Isolation." Each of us have claimed separate spheres of responsibility and denied that our roles ever coincided. Thus we in the seminaries have focused on professional education, without worrying about personal or spiritual formation. The church, on the other hand, has emphasized its right to decide who is to be ordained, often adding repetitive requirements and making seminarians jump through extraneous "hoops."

A third perspective might be called "Russian Roulette" or the "Wheel of Fortune." The recruitment and enlistment of future ordained and diaconal ministers has been by chance as both seminary and church have operated with the illusion of an overabundance of highly qualified persons for the ministry. The seminary has overprofessionalized ministry as a career, and the church has often neglected lifting the call of Christ to ministry.

At other times we seem to be "Independent Dancers," sharing the same dance floor of the church and world, but barely relating to each other as we gyrate alone "doing our own thing." Sometimes it doesn't seem that we even hear the same music. Our cooperation has been random, restricted, and reluctant.

My wife, Bonnie, is a licensed psychologist and reminds me that from a marriage counseling perspective it is a romantic mirage to believe there are "Perfect Relationships." She suggests unrealistic idealism can often create impractical expectations, unlikely to be achieved and leading to unnecessary disappointment. Many a home would be happier if people appreciated the fact that they have a "good enough" relationship or were "good enough" parents, rather than chastising themselves and each other in a quixotic quest for the perfect relationship. Thus in moving toward a new partnership between church and seminary, let us not pretend it will be a perfect relationship, but let us seek one "good enough" to meet the challenging needs we jointly face. Obviously we always must seek improvement—or "to go on to perfection" as John Wesley suggested—but let us concentrate on being "good enough" in some basic areas without engaging in utopian idealism.

In moving toward a new partnership between church and seminary, let us at least seek to be "good enough" colleagues that enmity might be replaced by amity, and invidious scapegoating might be displaced by imaginative cooperation. Let us ever avoid being "tossed to and fro and blown about by every wind of doctrine, by people's trickery, by their craftiness in deceitful scheming," but never fear "speaking the truth in love" to one another with the hope of growing "up in every way into him who is the head, into Christ." In the following chapters a new vision of ministerial education will be highlighted which illustrates how this new partnership might be manifested. May it serve as an invitation to consider other ways this "less than perfect" relationship might be enhanced.

CHAPTER THREE

A New Vision
of the Seminaries

....

"No one sews a piece of unshrunk cloth on an old cloak, for the patch pulls away from the cloak, and a worse tear is made. Neither is new wine put into old wineskins; otherwise, the skins burst, and the wine is spilled, and the skins are destroyed; but new wine is put into fresh wineskins, and so both are preserved."

MATTHEW 9:16-17

Since major league baseball came to Denver with the Colorado Rockies, I have become an ardent fan. My reading has expanded to the great philosophers of baseball like Satchel Paige, Casey Stengel, and Yogi Berra. They have offered us memorable insights into life such as: "Don't look back. Something may be gaining on you." "They say you can't do it, but remember, that doesn't always work." "The game isn't over till it's over." One of them, I am sure, also offered the profound prophecy that "the future ain't what it used to be!" Readers will please indulge my use of the latter phrase, illicit contraction included.

Changing Canons of Culture

Globally, we have come to accept the truth of this maxim almost daily. Truly, the future ain't what it used to be! The cataclysmic changes of recent years sometimes have almost paralyzed our emotional system. Adapting to rapid global and social change and adjusting to new visions of reality always proves to be a challenge.

When the Berlin Wall suddenly collapsed and Germany was reunified, how many of us even stopped to offer a prayer of thanks or lift a glass to toast this remarkable development? I had to search on page two of *The Denver Post* to find the unprecedented joint announcement that the Soviet Union and the United States had agreed on a treaty to destroy tens of thousands of conventional weapons in Europe. The treaty would result in the largest destruction of weapons in history. Swords were being beaten into plowshares! And Christians were practically silent! Our prayers were being answered, but many of us failed to whisper prayers of thanksgiving to God.

Suddenly the United Nations has been reactivated after years of slumber and elevated to the forefront of international affairs. The confrontation between the major powers has been dramatically diminished, but now throughout the world we discover ethnic fighting emerging. Sometimes it seems every tribe prefers its own tent, and tolerance for societal pluralism is dwindling. The United States finds itself in a political and military confrontation in small nations like Somalia and Haiti. Nuclear proliferation threatens. The peril of a divided Korea threatens. Often we are faced with Muslim rage and realities that we simply don't understand.

Change, of course, is the law of life. Some claim Adam paused as he was exiting the Garden of Eden and said, "Eve, we are living in a period of rapid social change!" Jesus discovered his disciples often were paralyzed by change. He told the twin parables of the patch of unshrunk cloth on an old robe and putting new wine into old wineskins (Matthew 9:16-17), as a way of emphasizing the revolutionary character of the new faith he was sharing. New truth cannot be forced into outdated traditions. God is creating a new world! The good news of the Kingdom cannot be contained in old forms.

What is different today is the radical speeding up of the tempo of global change that exists at the heart of the modern experience and helps shape the context and contours of our challenges in theological education now and in the future. A new vision of the seminaries—new wineskins for ministerial education—is imperative. The entry of a new information superhighway only enhances our awareness of this metamorphosis and prompts us to explore new ways of communicating the gospel of Jesus Christ.

Lynn White, Jr., spoke of the "changing canons of culture" in a book called *Frontiers of Knowledge*.[1] Canons, in this case, means accepted principles, rules, or normative standards of a culture. He suggests that the major canons or rules of our culture have in fact changed, or have begun to change. He lists seven changing canons, here is only one of his examples. He noted that

> Since the days of the Greeks our thinking has been framed within the canon of the Occident. This is the unexamined assumption that civilization par excellence is that of the Western tradition; ... All else—the epic spectacles of Peru and Mexico, of Islam, India, ... of China, Korea, and Japan, even that extraordinary Eastern Christendom of Byzantium and Russia—was either irrelevant or at best a cabinet of curiosities. ... Our image of the person is ceasing to assume tacitly that the white man is made peculiarly in the likeness of God.
>
> The canon of the Occident has been displaced by *the canon of the globe*. ... Few of us realize the extent to which our most ordinary actions and thoughts are being formed according to non-Occidental models.[2]

Neighbors in a Shrinking Global Village

Truly, the future ain't what it used to be. Unfortunately, however, much of theological education in our day still operates within the framework of the "canon of the Occident" without reference to Asia or Africa or Latin America. But both the world and the church have been changing.

When the twentieth century dawned, 85 to 90 percent of all Christians lived in the West. At the sunset of this millennium, 58 percent of all Christians will be living in the so-called "Third World" or "Two-thirds World." In 1900, 3 percent of Africa's population (or four million persons) were Christian; by the year 2000, nearly 50 percent (or 400 million persons) in Africa will be Christians. In Latin America there were 62 million Christians in 1900, and 400 million are expected in 2000. In South and East Asia there were 19 million Christians in 1900, and 225 million Christians are anticipated in 2000. Christianity has been more successful in winning adherents in the "Two-thirds World" than retaining them in Europe. Only one person in ten goes to church in Great Britain each Sunday, while in Scandinavia 90 percent of the population claims Lutheran church membership but only 5 percent enter churches on Sundays.

Christianity's center of gravity has shifted from the financially rich "One-third World" to the poorer "Two-thirds World."

A hundred years ago, 34 percent of the world's population was Christian. In the year 2000 it is anticipated 34 percent of the world's population will still be Christian, but the distribution of Christians and adherents to the other great world faiths will be different. There has been a revitalization and resurgence in other faiths as well. In the year 2000 it is projected that 19.2 percent of the world will be Muslim, 5.7 percent Buddhist, and 13.7 percent Hindu.[3]

Today we no longer live apart from one another but are literally neighbors in a shrinking global village. More Muslims live in America than Episcopalians, more Buddhists than Quakers, and so forth. There are some 896,078,000 Muslims in the world with 3,157,000 living in North America. But what do we really know about Muslim beliefs, culture, and lifestyle? Our American future won't imitate what used to be, and likewise the challenges pressing Christian theological education certainly aren't facsimiles of the past!

The canons or norms of culture have indeed changed. Seminaries now must have a vision of preparing persons for Christian ministry and other forms of religious leadership who have more than an Occidental or Western perspective. The canon or norm is now global and interreligious. The dominance of the "white man" must no longer prevail, and a new vision of gender, racial, and ethnic inclusiveness must predominate.[4] In this dynamic and incredibly challenging era, "new wineskins" for theological education are required, lest in Jesus words "the wine is spilled, and the skins are destroyed" (Matthew 9:16-17).

In an era of internationalism, we in the theological schools need ever to be aware of the propensity of tribalism in religion. Instead of embracing humanity and endorsing the richness of gifts God has given every people, culture, and religion, communities of faith often retreat into homogeneous and seemingly safe havens. For many the romance of ecumenism is over and the triumphalism of denominationalism is everywhere apparent. To prophetically teach and preach a global theology is to swim against the tribal tides of our time. Yet the global dimension of theological education must continually be reaffirmed and reappropriated.

A few years ago, Bishop K. H. Ting of China brought me a beautiful scroll to hang in my office. The Chinese calligraphy highlighted two words taken from the writings of Dr. Sun Yet Sin, the founder of China's first republic. Translated, these words mean: "Global love." Yes, it is global or universal love that we must teach and preach. It is the love of Christ that transcends every barrier, every nation, every race, every culture, and every people. It is the love of the good ship "Ecumene" that no time or trend can ever eliminate. It is the love of God and neighbor that underlies our reason for being in the business of theological education.

Globalization means different things to different persons and seminaries. Don S. Browning has noted four different perspectives on its meaning, with certain theological schools emphasizing certain dimensions more than others. First is an emphasis on evangelism, sharing the gospel with people in all nations. A second stresses ecumenism, which encourages greater cooperation and understanding among churches and people with different Christian theologies. Interreligious dialogue, the third dimension, emphasizes bridging the gaps between the world's major religions. The fourth interpretation focuses on social justice or human development issues, that is, seeking to improve the welfare of suffering people around the world.[5] In this and other books I have sought to embrace all four meanings of globalization as essential to the vision of the church and its seminaries.

The Vocation of a Theological School

What is God calling the theological schools in the age of pluralism and the new information superhighway to be and to do? This key question forces us to probe the vision and vocation of our theological schools in response to the context of globalization and the changing canons of culture. Vision and vocation flows from God and the continuing challenge requires discernment of the will of God at this time for theological education.

Does it make any difference where a seminary is located in how it understands its mission as an institution in preparing persons for Christian ministry? Should a seminary in St. Paul, Minnesota, have a different character to its ethos and curriculum than a theological school in St. Petersburg, Russia, or São Paulo, Brazil, or Singapore, or Zaire? Just as many churches and seminaries in postcolonial countries have discovered that their understanding of Christian ministry was more influenced by inherited European missionary models rather than by a contextual theology appropriate to their situation, so church and seminaries in the U.S. must question whether their vocational vision of mission and ministry has been predetermined by some inherited academic or even church model foreign to the soil where they exist and serve.[6]

Theological education must be simultaneously global and local, international and regional, urban and rural. An often repeated phrase of the French philosopher Jacques Ellul has become almost a cliché: "Think globally and act locally." It has become the watchword of efforts to globalize theological education. Seminary projects have blossomed to expand the student's global vision and to equip leaders for a faithful and effective ministry in an increasingly interdependent global village. In Max L. Stackhouse's words, "the vocation of Christian theological education is to prepare women and men to be theologians and ethicists in residence and in mission among the peoples of God in the multiple contexts around the globe."[7]

What has often been overlooked, however, says Robert A. Evans, is that "the mark of global conversion is local immersion."[8] True globalization means plunging into one's own neighborhood and region. The "salinization of mission" (i.e., "traveling over salt water") is not required.[9] God's mission exists on everyone's doorstep, not only in distant places. Admittedly, says Robert A. Evans, it is "more exotic and enticing to experience this transforming encounter with the other in India or Peru or South Africa. International exchange is often 'safer' since colleagues in those countries are neither as accessible to participants nor as persistent in their demands for mutuality as are brothers and sisters within our own cities,"[10] or I might add, our own rural region.

Ironically, mainline seminaries and their faculties sometimes are far more open for dialogue and cooperation with distant "evangelicals" than those next door or within their own denominations. Unfortunately, the same can be said of evangelical churches and seminaries. If "global love" doesn't begin at home, its genuineness remains open to question. In the 1960s when I marched for civil rights in Selma, Alabama, I heard that the local church did not welcome African Americans as members, though it supported missionaries to Africa! As a young seminarian, the hypocrisy haunted me, but parallel patterns persist today. Liberal theologians promoting interfaith dialogue sometimes have no patience for conversations with evangelicals. Evangelical Christians professing the love of Christ sometimes speak in the most condemning ways about "liberals" and/or homosexuals.

The question must be raised as to how each seminary responds to the poor and those treated as nonpersons in their own region. Harold J. Recinos critiques the globalization emphasis in theological education as being "a movement issuing forth from the compassionate ethics of a predominantly white middle class." It has advocated justice and human rights for persons in the Two-thirds World. It has often failed, however,

> to make connections with the poor of first world society who are overwhelmingly rooted in the inner cities of the nation. The concern for transformation has for the most part not moved middle-class Christians to identification with the vision of a renewed society held by Latinos, blacks, Asians, Arabs, Native Americans, and poor whites.[11]

Rural poverty is often heavily disguised. Hispanic migrant workers often suffer abuse and lack protection. The scandal of the status of Native Americans cannot be minimized. How is the rich diversity of persons of color being served by the seminary and being included in the faculty and curriculum? Has the seminary become divorced from understanding and ministry with white, ethnic, blue collar workers?[12] Are gays and lesbians an excluded minority? A globalization emphasis that incorporates a regional perspective seeks to be responsive and responsible to the complete mosaic of peoples and classes that constitute the neighborhood of a particular seminary. If all peoples are embraced within an area, then globalization could be a needed stimulus for renewing and revitalizing Christian mission and ministry.

The Minnesota Consortium of Theological Schools (composed of both "liberal" and "conservative" seminaries) has illustrated in recent years how to be both globally and locally concerned and committed. The seminaries have explored in depth the environmental and development crises being experienced in the Northern Plains. The onslaught of agribusiness, the globalization of transnational agricultural corporations, the neglected and unenlightened national and state farm policies, the relentless deterioration of the health of soil, water, forest and grassland resources, and demographic shifts have been included. These eco-justice issues cannot be ignored since they have a massive impact on the stability of rural communities, farm families, town businesses, churches, schools, medical services, and so forth. In such a context of crisis, theological education in this region cannot simply continue with "business as usual" but seeks to raise the consciousness of the churches and seminaries about the urgent conditions and circumstances it must address.

Imagine what might happen, as a result of these studies, if in the Northern Plains region (and elsewhere) seminary faculties, Protestant and Roman Catholic, liberal and evangelical, eventually spend their fall retreat times living in farming communities and worshiping in country churches? Think of seminary faculty, students, trustees, and administrators immersing themselves for a couple of weeks in both urban and rural settings? Envision them sleeping with the homeless of Minnesota on a freezing night, or joining a farmer's protest demonstration, or caring for persons living with AIDS?

Would Bible or theology or preaching be taught the same way during the next week? How would theology be taught differently or become more alive and relevant to students? How would the context and crisis have an impact on the understandings of the urgency of the gospel message and the meaning of the biblical, theological, or historical texts? For one thing, it might cause a seismic shift in understanding and perception of who the diverse people are that live and work in the region. For example, as United Methodist Bishop Roy I. Sano has observed:

Many of our farmers on the plains listen to the price of their grains on the world market before leaving home for work at 5:30 in the morning. They listen to international news as they plow the fields in the air-conditioned cabs of their combines. These farmers have a picture of the movement of their grains on interstate highways and train tracks across the U.S. They are familiar with the shipping lanes that connect major ports, sending their products around the globe. Agriculturists in America's heartland are hardly parochial and uninformed about the global networks in which they live and work.[13]

Curriculum and the way it is communicated would change, not because it had been mandated from an administrative or trustee hierarchy, but because faculty had new visions and experiences of God's mission in the world. The vocational challenge of theological education today is to attempt to discern the Divine will and way amid changing world conditions and along the emerging new information superhighway.

Constructing Regional Theologies

Global contextualization encourages constructing local or regional theologies. As Robert J. Schreiter has noted, it is "becoming increasingly evident that the theologies once thought to have a universal, and even enduring or perennial character (such as neo-scholastic Thomism in Roman Catholicism or neo-orthodoxy in Protestantism) were but regional expressions of certain cultures."[14] Christian theology is being freed from the chains of Aristotelian, Latin, and Teutonic thought prisons.

Roman Catholic theologian Hans Küng once declared that the old assimilation method of missions aimed at making persons into Europeans before inviting them to be Christians![15] But today Christians are being encouraged everywhere to reflect upon their experience and the Scriptures within the context of where they live and work. This is not to ignore the role of the professional or academic theologian, but it is to draw those rich resources into a creative community context of theologizing. In a rural American context, for example, Frederick Kirschenmann urged Minnesota's theological schools to teach a theology of "expectation" that "could transform rural perceptions from failure to self-esteem and empowerment." He asked the seminaries to sensitize "rural ministers to the bond between good local culture and ecological caring—standing on the side of economic justice for rural communities, and encouraging those communities to identify and mobilize their own strengths."[16]

The Sri Lankan Jesuit Aloysius Pieris contends that today's missional church "must step into the baptismal waters of Asian religion and pass through passion and death on the cross of Asian poverty."[17] Likewise, today's missional ministry in the United States must step into the baptismal waters of Northern Plains culture and multicultural urban Miami and feel the cross of contemporary crisis and pain before the church can know the experience of resurrection and new life. Whether we are going as missionary pastors to rural or urban America or to Buddhist Asia or to contemporary Africa, we must go "expecting" to find Christ already active in that culture. Seminarians must be introduced to the

> belief that the risen Christ's salvific activity in bringing about the kingdom of God is already going on before our arrival. From a missionary perspective there would be no conversion if the grace of God had not preceded the missionary and opened the hearts of those who heard.[18]

An incarnational theology, rooted in the scriptural confession that "God so loved the world that he gave his only Son" (John 3:16) emphasizes the concrete and the particular, the regional and the local, as well as the universal and global. Theological education, at its best, teeters ever on a tightrope as it seeks to introduce and blend these divergent dimensions together for the seminarian and the church.

Learning from Two-thirds World Partners

At this point, seminaries in the United States can benefit from the experience and instruction of partners in theological education in other countries, particularly from the "Two-thirds World." Christians who have struggled through the dominance of the Western model of theological education provide insights regarding Christ and culture that may not be readily evident to those enmeshed in historic structures. As North American churches struggle with the problem of financing full-time pastors, and seminaries face insufficient scholarship programs to support full-time studies for students, they might look at different approaches. Since "the future ain't what it used to be" in terms of multiculturalism and multireligious communities in the United States, new ways of thinking and teaching are in demand.

Traditional theological education, notes Emilio Castro, former General Secretary of the World Council of Churches, has been dominated by a professional model that doesn't fit most small struggling churches around the world. Even if they chose this paradigm, they couldn't afford the salaries, benefits, and lifestyle normally associated with professionalism. Second, the full-time model of professional ministry doesn't work well in many cultures. The resources of the church simply can't support such an approach. Third, students have no way to support themselves and their families during full-time studies, and scholarships are insufficient. Fourth, seminary education typically alienates persons from the very culture they profess to serve.[19] Too often the educational system has become a barrier for Christian ministry. No easy solutions exist in this regard. Not long ago I read a report from China, saying that new seminary graduates educated in the cities of Beijing, Shanghai, and Nanjing often now are misfits in rural communities. The United Methodist bishop of Eurasia told me that the first graduates of a nascent ecumenical seminary all planned to stay in Moscow!

Programs of theological education by extension, designed not only for clergy but for all God's people have been pioneered in places like Latin America and the Caribbean, as well as Africa and Asia. Ministerial formation has, of necessity and choice, taken different options than what has been traditionally done in Europe and the United States. Distance education, as envisioned now in the age of the information superhighway, has been happening for years via correspondence courses, nonresidential seminars, itinerant professors, and so forth. In places of extreme poverty, these are likely to be the only alternatives for years to come, as the worlds of computers and communications will remain too costly. When a United Methodist agency proposed providing every Native

American pastor in the U.S. a fax machine, I heard the resident bishop of the Oklahoma Area explode: "First, they need a telephone!" In places lacking phones, or the financial resources to pay for them, fax machines and modems are but elitist inventions and playthings.

A recent book, *Ministerial Formation in a Multifaith Milieu,* describes both the dilemmas and dimensions of preparing pastors and laity in a world of religious pluralism.[20] Some seminaries teach other world religions with the purpose of discovering their defects and developing strategies for evangelism and conversion. Others teach with a view toward understanding and appreciating the spiritual strengths of Islam, Buddhism, Hinduism, and so forth. Dare a Christian seminary have a Buddhist teaching his or her faith, or must it always be a Christian who ultimately denies the tenets of Buddhism?

As a boy of six in a very small town church on the prairie of South Dakota, a returning missionary from China first awakened within me an interest in globalization. While in college at Dakota Wesleyan University, I ventured forth for a junior year of study at Madras Christian College in Tambaram, India. After a year of encircling the globe, making friends with Hindus, Muslims, Buddhists, and Christians in some twenty-three countries, I stopped at Boston University to visit The School of Theology. What impressed me most at the time was the presence of a Hindu scholar on the faculty, Professor Amita Chakavarty. A year later I returned with the purpose of becoming an expert in world religions so that I could assist in developing the synthesis of the great faiths and the world could be unified by one great religion! After the first semester, I realized this was an illusory goal. I would never manage to understand even a small slice of Protestantism much less grasp the global history and theology of religions! What I did learn from Walter G. Muelder and others was that the church of Jesus Christ must always be cross-cultural, transnational, and ecumenical. Witnessing for Christ, interreligious dialogue, and struggling for justice were integral to theological education. Boston University School of Theology was ahead of its time in theological education as it embodied the global concept of appreciating and appropriating from all cultures, religions, and peoples.

Personally, what amazes me some thirty years later is that major universities in the United States—like Yale, Duke, Emory and others—still support essentially Protestant professional seminaries, with minimal attention to other religious traditions. Graduate schools of religion exist in the universities, but imagine having law schools that only catered to one major tradition or medical schools in these universities that focused only on limited specialties. Yet with few exceptions these major divinity schools will not have faculty members who are members of other religious faiths. Just the idea of having a person not of the Christian faith—no matter how ethically upright or spiritually committed—is beyond the theological and emotional radar of most theological educators in denominational schools. A certain religious parochialism is inherent in contemporary theological education structures. Far from being revolutionary centers as alleged by Thomas C. Oden and others, they are essentially conservative places, transmitting and upholding the historic traditions of the faith.

Nine Present Trends Among Seminaries

Nine trends demonstrate how "the future ain't what it used to be" in today's seminaries. The days of prejudice, parochialism, and provincialism are numbered. Until the 1960s civil rights revolution, many major Protestant seminaries in the South were segregated. In recent times, the anachronism of white male dominance of faculties, administration, and trustees has been slowly changing. A seminary serving exclusively one denomination has become rare indeed. Numerous trends toward diversity could be highlighted, but let me underscore only nine. Others could be added.

First, the gender barrier has been broken and women students have been welcomed into the seminaries in increasing numbers. After centuries of sexism, the church that proclaimed "there is no longer male and female; for all of you are one in Christ Jesus" (Gal. 3:28) finally was forced to open its doors of opportunity to women as well as men. Even Roman Catholics and conservative evangelical denominations have begun to provide more opportunities for women, while still resisting ordination. But the ordination of women has become an irreversible tide, and, in my judgment, it is just a matter of time before all God's people are accorded their proper status in the church. Over the years I have told more than one church group resistant to women clergy that they should not take their complaints to us in the seminaries but to God who has called them into ministry! In 1992–93 women compose 31.1 percent of all students in accredited seminaries, compared to 10.2 percent twenty years ago.[21] A higher percentage attend mainstream seminaries. For example, women comprise 41.5 percent of enrollment in United Methodist theological schools versus 31.8 percent a decade ago.

Second, women are emerging as tenured faculty, senior administrators, and influential trustees. For decades seminaries, even those who thought of themselves as "liberal," had no women faculty or senior administrators. Only in recent years has this discriminatory pattern been broken. There is a certain irony that white male professors like Oden are now suddenly so worried about the dangers of tenure as women begin to benefit from the protection of academic freedom and security that men like Oden and others have enjoyed for many years. It used to be said, and rightfully so, that if a woman wanted to be a college president, then she first had to become a nun! Now more women are being selected as presidents in colleges and universities, though seminaries still lag seriously behind. In 1993 only 5.5 percent of the seminaries had women presidents, and 11.6 percent had female deans serving the 219 Protestant, Roman Catholic, and Orthodox seminaries accredited by the Association of Theological Schools.[22] Women still are a minority on Boards of Trustees, but their numbers are increasing.

Third, the number of persons of color as students and faculty is slowly changing. Progress at overcoming centuries of white racism in church and culture proves to be painstakingly slow. The percentage of ethnic/racial students in A.T.S. accredited theological schools in 1992–93 was 8.8 percent African American, 2.6 percent Hispanic, 4.9 percent Pacific/Asian, .2 percent Native American, and .3 percent international. Twenty years ago it was 3.2 percent African American, 0.8 percent Hispanic, 1.1 percent Pacific/Asian, with no records on Native Americans and international students.[23]

In terms of the faculty, the percentages for 1993–94 are as follows: 4.7 percent African American, 2.0 percent Hispanic, .08 percent Native American, 2.2 percent Asian, and .3 percent international.[24] Statistics are not available for persons of color serving as senior administrators and trustees, but the numbers are embarrassingly low for churches and seminaries giving lip service to inclusiveness.

Fourth, today's seminary students are older than in previous generations. Second and third career persons are entering the ministry. Younger students (between the ages of twenty and twenty-nine) are declining in seminaries related to the Association of Theological Schools, while older students (between the age of forty and forty-nine) are increasing the most across all degree programs.[25] Barriers against ageism have crumbled somewhat in the churches and persons often are entering the profession later in life.

Overall seminary student enrollment statistics in the United States and Canada reveal that women are older than men, with 29.4 percent of the men over age forty and 42.8 percent of the women over age forty.[26] Recent statistics indicate the average age of seminarians in United Methodist schools is thirty-five years old versus twenty-five years old in 1968.[27] This has brought to the campus a new level of maturity and experience, since many of these persons have long been active lay members of congregations. Older students also sometimes bring with them the marks and scars of current culture: "unstable and broken family relationships; experimentation with drugs, alcohol, and sexuality; the strengths and weaknesses of living in a materialistic, competitive, and highly individualistic culture, and so on."[28]

Fifth, seminary curriculums are being revised to reflect more global and ecumenical perspectives. Teaching denominational history, theology, and polity continues to be important, but President Carnegie Samuel Calian of Pittsburgh Theological Seminary notes that increased attention is being directed to transcending denominational parochialism and helping students understand the ecumenical, global nature of the church.[29] Requiring texts and reading lists that expose students to a variety of theological perspectives, as well as having been written by persons of both genders and various racial/ethnic backgrounds, is being emphasized. The presence of international faculty and students is imperative. For example, thanks to the endowed Louise Iliff Visiting Professors program at The Iliff School of Theology, our students have had an opportunity to study with faculty in the past ten years from Costa Rica, Argentina, Uruguay, Bolivia, Hong Kong, Kenya, South Africa, India, and Brazil. Faculty from U.S. schools have been experiencing immersions in other cultures and are seeking out special relationships and partnerships with seminaries in other countries.

Sixth, in the past twenty years, as the world has become more of a neighborhood, theological schools unfortunately have tended to become more regional in their student bodies. This runs somewhat counter to trend five. For various reasons, but especially because of economic necessity, more and more students remain in their own region for their theological education. Opportunities for student parishes, working spouses, children in school, and so forth all contribute to this trend. Not to be overlooked is the fact that seminaries across the country have increased in quality over the past thirty years. The negative dimension of this drift has been the concentration of graduates from one seminary in particular conferences or dioceses. As a rural South Dakotan, it broadened my vision of mission and ministry by studying in Boston and working with youth gangs in an inner-city African American church. Now a large percentage of seminarians never leave South Dakota to be exposed to the diversity of the church and culture elsewhere. The same thing happens in Oklahoma, Iowa, Kentucky, Massachusetts, and other places.

Trends seven and eight remain problematic for the seminaries, because of real or perceived opposition from the churches. *Trend seven reflects the religious diversity of faculty—the inclusion of persons of other faiths on the faculty.* The use of adjunct faculty, teaching on a part-time basis, has long been utilized in the seminaries to compensate for the lack of expertise in world religions. Visiting Jewish rabbis have been common. Recently, however, a few seminaries have dared to break from this exclusive pattern and invited persons of other major religious faiths to join the core faculty in tenured positions. Their numbers remain very limited and no known statistics are available. Iliff, for example, has a Buddhist teaching philosophy of religion and a Jew teaching biblical studies. Other United Methodist seminaries have also added Jewish faculty, but the practice is not very widespread, despite a renewed emphasis on the importance of interfaith dialogue. With persons and communities of Judaism, Buddhism, Islam, and Hinduism at every church's and seminary's doorstep, the possibilities of interreligious conflict or cooperation can emerge anywhere, and seminary graduates must be prepared for this new situation and ministry wherever they are.

The eighth trend is generally a taboo subject, namely the presence of openly gay and lesbian students in seminary. The strong condemnation of homosexuality by Roman Catholicism and most mainline and evangelical Protestant churches makes the possibilities of ordained ministry of such persons very limited. Yet openly gay and lesbian persons seek out seminaries for their spiritual and theological development as well as to fulfill their sense of calling into Christ's ministry. Seminaries, in particular, are caught in the crossfire between their sponsoring churches and their students.

A few mainline and university-based seminaries explicitly welcome gays and lesbians, but most find the subject far too controversial for open discussion or acknowledgment. Seminaries that do demonstrate hospitality to all persons realize they have an educational obligation to inform gay and lesbian students of the stances various denominations take toward ordination and ministry. Quick change of these policies is unlikely and students need to understand the dynamics of church politics. Tempting as it may be to ignore the deep differences between Christians on these issues, seminaries are obligated to help persons understand why Christians are so divided in regard to homosexuality. One resource in this educational process is a book I edited with Sally B. Geis, *Caught in the Crossfire: Helping Christians Debate Homosexuality.* In it essayists with clashing perspectives on the Bible, science, ordination, same-sex unions, and so forth, present their views, and the editors seek to clarify points of agreement and disagreement.[30]

Whether the number of gay and lesbian students is actually increasing is questionable; the actual numbers may be no different than thirty years ago. The "homosexualization of theological education" that critics imagine certainly represents an exaggeration, but the presence of gay and lesbian persons does indeed enrich the diversity of contemporary seminaries. What is increasing has been the fact that they are Christians who are open and proud gay men and lesbians. Straight Christians, joining in solidarity with their gay brothers and lesbian sisters, seek to change the attitudes and policies of their churches.

Also changing the character of contemporary seminaries is a *ninth trend: students enter seminary with limited previous studies in religion and tend to study on a part-time basis, as they seek to earn enough money to pay for their seminary education.* Previous generations of seminarians were more likely to have completed formal college training in religion and the humanities, been residential students at the seminary, and worked part-time while they studied full-time.

Lack of previous training forces changes in the seminary curriculum. Entering seminarians, in Marjorie H. Suchocki's words, often know little "biblical content, let alone biblical scholarship; they are ignorant of Christian history in either its positive or negative dimensions, and they know little of theology beyond credal phrases. This means, of course, that all seminary courses must presume a bare entry-level knowledge, so that we begin 'master's' study at an introductory stage."[31]

Since church support and scholarship aid has not kept up with the ever-increasing costs of theological education, the burden of financing schooling has fallen on the student. In order to pay for family, tuition, books, housing, food, and so forth, students have been forced sometimes to work and borrow excessively. A recent study discovered that 48 percent of the 1991 Master of Divinity graduates did borrow, about half borrowed less than $10,000 (25 percent of the total graduates) and about one-third owed from $10,000 to $20,000 (or 15 percent of all graduates).[32] While debt loads of existing seminarians have not reached a crisis point overall, certain graduates clearly have exceeded what is desirable as they begin low paying pastorates or other positions in the church.

In an age of commuter students, extension classes, and evening classes, creating "community" conducive to spiritual formation becomes more problematic. Faculties are faced with the perplexities of how to structure the curriculum and how to teach this new generation of students. Higher head counts and lower full-time student numbers mean administrators are faced with higher costs as the demands for more services increases.

A new vision of the seminaries must take into account these nine trends which serve to illustrate the truth that "the future ain't what it used to be." To use Jesus' analogies, theological schools can neither expect to put new patches on old institutional clothing and expect them to work, nor can they expect that the fresh vitality and fermenting diversity of persons engaged in ministerial education can be contained in the old seminary wineskins. Some will lament the loss of the past, but many others will affirm the good news that the future is likely to be better, as all God's people benefit from theological education and prepare for Christian ministry in today's world.

These trends also serve as an introduction to the next two chapters, which explore visions of the prophetic servant and redemptive community dimensions of theological education in the life of the church and society. Servanthood doesn't mean just promoting the status quo, but can mean pushing for change as mandated by the gospel. The controversial character of some of these trends illustrates the possibly subversive role of the seminary as well as how conflict, controversy, and progress are related.

CHAPTER FOUR

Theological Education
as a Subversive Activity

Put on the whole armor of God, so that you may be able to stand against the wiles of the devil. For our struggle is not against enemies of blood and flesh, but against the rulers, against the authorities, against the cosmic powers of this present darkness, against the spiritual forces of evil in the heavenly places.

EPHESIANS 6:11-12

Amid seminary reports from around the globe at the 1986 Theological Education Convocation of World Methodism in Nairobi, Kenya, a black South African rose and spoke in a very quiet, almost matter-of-fact tone of voice. He told how his seminary community had been constantly harassed by the South African apartheid government. He described how at one point forty-seven students and staff were arrested. He detailed how police officials had ransacked the theological library and took books they thought were inappropriate. Once 200 people had gathered at the gates of the school and demanded to take over the campus.

The speaker reported that the seminary recently had been invaded at 3:00 A.M. by thirty-five armed vehicles and some 300 military persons. They searched the homes of the faculty and the rooms of all 121 students. One student was detained without charges for ten days. This black South African theological educator quietly closed his presentation by noting that his own daughter was at that time experiencing her fourth week of prison detention without charges.

The drama and trauma of listening to this account prompted me to ask the following questions. What would theological education in the United States be like if it was experiencing the threat and harassment of the government? How would our life be different if we were struggling for survival against hostile state forces? Would we speak or act differently if what we said or did was viewed as dangerously threatening to the status quo? Is theological education at its best a subversive activity?

Citadels of Conservatism

In many respects it is almost impossible for us to entertain these questions in any lively and meaningful fashion. Theological schools in the United States generally are viewed as citadels of conservatism in our culture. Far from attacking them, the society basically ignores their existence, even protecting them through favorable tax legislation. Periodically, particular church bodies, such as the Roman Catholic Church and the Southern Baptist Convention,[1] become fearful of the subversive character of their seminaries, but the state itself or society in general seldom becomes exercised over what, if anything, is happening within the theological schools.

Without question seminaries do have a major commitment to conserving activities. In a culture that often prizes the innovative and the new at the expense of tradition and history, theological educators are firm in their insistence on remembering and reappropriating an ancient biblical and theological heritage. The preservation and transmission of that heritage is fundamental to the seminary's existence.

Symbolic of this emphasis on the preservation of the past is the central role of the library in theological education. In the midst of a transient, disposable, "golden arches" culture, the library is a conservatizing institution that values the accumulated wisdom of the past. Libraries serve as the bedrock of theological teaching, learning, and research. A major proportion of a school's resources are spent each year in purchasing, maintaining, and circulating books and periodicals. In the age of the new information superhighway, libraries are becoming the control center of communication, with libraries linked together by computers.

In addition to the conserving function of the library, the seminary is viewed generally as a conservative institution within society, since its primary purpose is to prepare persons for ministry within the church. The bulk of seminary graduates are hardly revolutionaries, in that they serve established structures of church and society.

In many respects this proves to be an indictment, not a compliment, of the role theological seminaries play in our society. Exceptions, of course, can and should be noted. In the civil rights struggle, Martin Luther King, Jr. stimulated the prophetic role for many clergy and seminarians. But, with painful reluctance, I have to acknowledge that the image of the prophet has always been a sociologically "marginal" metaphor of ministry in the history of Christian communities of faith. The special circumstances of the 1960s and the 1970s may have given prominence to the prophetic role, but evidence clearly indicates that most laity and clergy were not reflective of this image in their daily witness and work.

Seminaries have reinforced this conserving function by emphasizing the professional model of ministry. While perhaps not intending to slight the prophetic dimension, the professional perspective has had a tendency to reduce ministry to tasks, to make ministry more a career than a calling, and to encourage an employee mentality more concerned with job descriptions and pensions than evangelism and mission. Professionalism may domesticate God's priests into hired functionaries or mere institutional employees. Personally, I believe that *when theological education moves beyond professionalism to more biblically and theologically based metaphors, the possibilities for subverting the status quo in church and society are more promising.* In two other books, *Contemporary Images of Christian Ministry* (Abingdon, 1989), and *A Conspiracy of Goodness* (Abingdon, 1992), I have sought to stimulate such imagistic thinking. Examples are "wounded healers in a community of the compassionate," "servant leaders in a servant church," "political mystics in a prophetic community," "a covenant of global gardeners," "a company of star throwers," and so on.[2]

Seeds of Subversion

Embedded within this conserving function of theological education, however, are the seeds of revolt, reform, revolution, and

75

even subversion. Vincent Harding, Iliff's professor of religion and social transformation, once remarked that "the trouble with playing with holy fire is that you can get burned!"

As conservative as libraries may appear, they often historically have been the spark for dynamic changes in thought and action. The medieval monasteries preserved the lamp of learning for the Western world. The Protestant Reformation library learnings of Martin Luther, John Calvin, and John Wesley proved subversive of the religious establishments of their time. Charles Darwin and Karl Marx launched major revolutions in science and politics from obscure library corners of the British Museum. Is it no wonder then that South African apartheid authorities feared seminary libraries?

Churches and seminaries potentially can be very threatening to oppressive powers and principalities. If they follow the instruction of Ephesians 6:11-12 and "put on the whole armor of God," they can "stand against the wiles of the devil . . . against the rulers, against the authorities, against the cosmic powers of this present darkness, against the spiritual forces of evil in the heavenly places." Let two illustrations—the Bible and the doctrine of the Resurrection—suffice to show how threatening and challenging church and seminary can potentially be.

Threatened by the Bible

In the minds of most people, ranking close to the library as a conserving activity is the teaching of the Bible. In every seminary, both mainstream and evangelical, biblical studies has a prominent position in the curriculum and requirements. It would not be difficult to demonstrate how Scripture has been used to sanctify the status quo or to oppress women and minorities. Yet it also can be argued that *the faithful transmission of God's Word certifies theological education as a subversive activity.* In the words of an Old Testament scholar, Walter Brueggemann, "the church in America doesn't have to decide whether it is going to engage in subversive activity. What the church in America really has to decide is whether it is going to read the Bible."[3]

Thank God circumstances in South Africa have now dramatically been transformed. A new day of democracy has dawned. Christian laity and clergy helped overthrow the chains of apartheid. Some church agencies and a few seminaries joined in refusing to invest endowments in firms doing any type of business with South Africa. A leader in that costly struggle, Anglican Archbishop Desmond Tutu has noted that when white people first came to Africa, the Africans had the land and the whites had the Bible. Tutu says the whites said, "Hello, hello" and the blacks responded "Hello." And then they said, "Let us pray." "So we dutifully shut our eyes, and when we opened them, we discovered they had the land and we had the Bible!" Waving his Bible before a cheering congregation during the revolutionary times, Tutu shouted, "We are taking the Bible seriously, because when you came and you gave us this, you gave us one of the most subversive things in a situation of oppression and injustice. . . . And so we tell the South African government, hey, the book that you should have banned long ago is the Bible, but you are too late, too late!"[4]

The 1993 Nobel Peace Prize winner, Rigoberta Menchu, reports in her autobiography that the Bible has been the "main weapon" for the self-defense of Guatemalan Indian communities against violent repression. She tells how they related biblical images of inspiration to their contemporary Indian culture. The men identified with Moses leading his people from oppression via the Exodus, the women focused on Judith slaying the king, and children imitated the shepherd boy David conquering Goliath. Their intense study of Bible stories and psalms helped them become equipped in self-defense against the brutal military forces. Further study convinced them, in Rigoberta Menchu's words:

> That being a Christian means thinking of our brothers around us, and that every one of our Indian race has the right to eat. This reflects what God . . . said, that on this earth we have a right to what we need. The Bible was our principal text for study as Christians and it showed us what the role of a Christian is . . . . We realized that it is not God's will that we should live in suffering, that God did not give us that destiny, but that men on earth have imposed this suffering, poverty, misery and discrimination on us.[5]

Joyce Hill of the United Methodist General Board of Global Ministries tells the story of how Julio Barreiro of Montevideo, Uruguay was arrested in the mid-1970s.[6] A lawyer and Methodist layman, he asked his wife to bring him three things: a change of underwear ("I will need it where I am"), an Agatha Christie novel ("To forget where I am"), and the Bible ("To remember whose I am"). Prison authorities did not permit him to have the Bible. Scripture was considered too subversive, since phrases like "I will lift up mine eyes unto the hills, from whence cometh my help" (Psalm 121:1) obviously refers to guerrillas!

Threatened by the Resurrection

Teaching the historical beliefs and doctrines of the church certainly could be classified as a conservative activity of the seminary. Central to the life of every theological school is the critical and creative reappropriation of the basic faith convictions that have motivated and sustained Christians through the centuries. This has always been and remains a fundamental function of the seminary. Along with transmitting the Scriptures, the teaching of theology and church history always represents core commitments of seminaries.

One disservice Thomas C. Oden has rendered in his writings and speeches has been to give the impression that theological schools are somehow ahistorical and antagonistic to historical theology. Examine any seminary curriculum, however, and one will discover numerous courses devoted to understanding not just the first five centuries of the Christian movement, but *all twenty centuries.* Faithful faculty seek to bring the best intellectual insights to their research, study, and teaching. Thus the transmission of these teachings and doctrines is not done in a simplistic fashion appropriate perhaps for a beginning Sunday school, but fitting for a graduate school committed not only to excellence but the pursuit of truth.

In the rich history of the church it is evident that even the most basic doctrines of the faith have always been open to various interpretations and understandings. Perceptions of God have varied within the Christian community. What it means to love one's neighbor has resulted in divergent perspectives. The meaning of Jesus Christ has resulted in numerous Christologies over the centuries. Theologian Delwin Brown, drawing attention to William A. Clebsch's study of *Christianity in European History,* notes that while Christians over five historical periods have held in common "Jesus Christ as savior and model of righteousness . . . the Jesus who endured throughout appeared in such varied roles amidst such diverse experiences that Clebsch says one should really speak of different 'Christs' and different 'Christianities.' "[7]

Basic doctrines have metaphorical power that go beyond simple rational discussion and reasoning. For example, the resurrection of Jesus, the Christ, evokes varieties of theological interpretation ranging from empirical reality to symbolism, but its sustaining and correcting power within the Christian community is beyond question.

Julia Esquivel, an exiled Guatemalan poet and lay theologian, has long struggled for human rights in her beloved country. She writes of the horror of human rights violations, the impoverishment of the indigenous peoples, the tragic disparity of the rich North and the poor South, and the agonizing gap between the way the world is and what God intended. In a famous poem entitled "They Have Threatened Us with Resurrection," she recalls one of the many massacres that have killed more than 100,0000 Guatemalans:

> What keeps us from sleeping
> is that they have threatened us with resurrection!
> Because at each nightfall
> though exhausted from the endless inventory
> of killings since 1954,
> yet we continue to love life
> and do not accept their death!

Amid death and destruction, Guatemalan Christians have affirmed the hope of the Resurrection and denied death its victory. Esquivel's invitation is to:

Accompany us then on this vigil
and you will know what it is to dream!
You will then know
how marvelous it is
to live threatened with Resurrection!

To dream awake,
to keep watch asleep,
to live while dying
and to already know oneself
resurrected![8]

The experience and metaphor of the Resurrection has been repeatedly expressed by Christians in the People's Republic of China. Despite years of oppression, persecution, and closure to the outside world, the church overcame these crucifixion experiences and kept the faith alive. In fact, when missionaries were expelled in 1949 by the communists, Protestants numbered about 700,000. By the late 1980s membership was conservatively estimated between three and four million persons with new congregations being established daily. New seminaries emerged across the country as Christians sought desperately to prepare pastors. Truly they understand themselves as a Resurrected Body of Christ.

The revolutionary hope of the Resurrection means restless impatience with the status quo—both in the church and culture. Once the early Christians experienced the hope of the Resurrection—the triumph of God in human life—they overcame their moral inertia and became morally involved. As Jurgen Moltmann has written: "Whoever is sent through Easter into History with a great Hope can no longer be satisfied with an anxious affirmation of the status quo in the world, but is called to transform the world through suffering and obedience."[9]

Behold the Turtle

Seminaries are always a subversive threat to churches and society, if they are faithful to the gospel and the pursuit of truth.

The threat of teaching the Bible and doctrines like the Resurrection are but two examples. Seminaries need to incarnate and witness to the prophetic tradition of Christianity by demonstrating a courage to risk and to lead—to be on the cutting edge of theological education. Being "avant garde" or intellectually experimental sounds creative and progressive. The problem, however, with being on the "cutting edge" is that one is likely to encounter resistance, get slashed, and end up bleeding a bit! There is peril in living on the edge—breakthroughs in theology or in any other field are never made without risk. Tension, conflict and controversy are inherent in progress.[10]

Academic freedom remains the guardian of the seminary's soul from political correctness advocates of both the left and the right. Political correctness, be it the liberal version championing its various causes or the conservative version upholding its various traditions, ever seeks to undermine the quest for truth and to impose its own absolute certainties.

Watching a performance of William Shakespeare's *The Merchant of Venice* recently, I was reminded how politically incorrect this classic could be judged. Surely its portrayal of the Jewish merchant was offensive, but likewise the penalty imposed upon him of converting to Christianity was outrageous. But to censor Shakespeare, or presumptuously attempt to upgrade this drama to match current sensibilities would be to jeopardize its insights into the human condition and to deprive oneself of the power of a play that has had enduring significance for generations.

A threat to freedom of speech and academic freedom now exists in many university and seminary classrooms. In more conservative atmospheres, faculty can sometimes be penalized or even dismissed for advocating doctrines or ideas outside loyalty oaths prescribed for all teachers. Advocating gay and lesbian rights can be dangerous to their professional lives. In more liberal environments, for example, the quest to end verbal sexual harassment has sometimes led to restrictions on freedom of speech and severe penalties for faculty members. A New Testament professor and former dean at Chicago Theological Seminary, Graydon Snyder, was placed on probation, ordered to apologize, and instructed to take remedial therapy, following an investigation of a female student complaint. In a $420,000 suit filed by Snyder against the seminary, he claims the alleged offense was his 1992 use of a story from the ancient Jewish Talmud which he had been using for thirty-four years to illustrate the dangers of seeking to distinguish between morally appropriate and inappropriate uses of language, and the potential "chilling effect" certain good causes, like ending verbal sexual harassment, can have on academic freedom and critical theological inquiry.[11]

Every theological school needs to ask where it is located in the "geography of faith." From the perspective of the atlas, we know where a school is physically located, but how do we map the school in the configuration of ideas and theology. The issue is where a particular seminary stands, what is its historic identity, and how can it best contribute to the education of persons for Christian ministry and other forms of religious leadership?

It is always more comfortable to stand in the center. Every institution is tempted to be cautiously centrist. Harvard psychiatrist Robert Coles says all institutions are plagued by these problems. He says, "Don't we always move from the radical critic or dissenter—be he Christ, be he Luther—to . . . institutional consolidations, then to a serious decline of the radical spirit with a parallel rise in cautiousness and institutional rigidity?"[12]

For many years I had a poster of a turtle prominently displayed in my office at home. To sit in the president's chair is to know a seemingly endless cycle of conflict and controversy. Every decision you make someone is sure to see as a decision against them. It is quite impossible to please all of one's constituents all of the time. No budget ever meets everyone's needs or wants. For an institution to move ahead, it is sometimes necessary to make hard decisions that are unpopular and misunderstood. For one who cherishes love and harmony as much as I do, there is often unspeakable personal pain and heartache. Thus, the saying on the poster has always been a simple but important reminder to me: "Behold the turtle: it only makes progress when it sticks its neck out!"

A Case Study of Conflict, Controversy, and Progress

The story of many American seminaries could be shared as illustrative of conflict, controversy, and progress. Since I best know its story, let me share The Iliff School of Theology in Denver, Colorado, as a case study. It would not be inaccurate to say that the school was founded amid conflict and controversy. People were upset when the Iliff family insisted that the University of Denver be moved from downtown into what was perceived as the countryside because the Iliffs wanted to start a new seminary. When the first president, Bishop Henry White Warren, espoused evolution, just a few years after Darwin's findings, he certainly did not win widespread approval from cautious clerics and conservative churches.

Sometimes when I despair with what journalists report, all I have to do is turn back the pages of history. On June 5, 1889, *The Rocky Mountain Herald* was upset because Bishop Henry White Warren had caused the resignation of the chancellor of the University of Denver, Dr. David H. Moore. The newspaper defended Moore, saying "he has more true Christianity in his make up than a thousand high salaried hypocrites such as Bishop Warren, and the day is not far distant when it will be fully demonstrated. Dr. Moore did not marry for money." (The reference to marriage was a form of "negative campaigning," suggesting that the Bishop had married the rich widow of John Wesly Iliff because of money, not love!)

The next year in 1890 when the Iliff family had Iliff closed temporarily in order to separate it from the University of Denver, *The Rocky Mountain News* reported a pamphlet saying that Bishop and Mrs. Warren had "pursued a torturous and deceptive course in the closing . . . and one unfair and unjust to the faculty." In an article entitled the "Bishop's House Is Torn Up," the writer declared that

> a discharge from a Krupp gun, landed in the midst of the peaceful prairies of University Park would hardly have raised such a turmoil. It is a silent uproar, however. The good Methodists of University Park discussed the pamphlet under their breath, in the dead of night, after the lights are out, and the curtains down, for all University Park dwells beneath the eaves of the sanctuary of the bishop's house.

Yes, conflict and controversy marked the birth and beginning of The Iliff School of Theology. Whether the good Methodists of

University Park cowered at night in fear is questionable, but no doubt there were expressions of agony and anguish. Hindsight, however, reveals that the Iliff family had appropriate vision and courage. By extricating the school from the future financial problems of the University of Denver, and establishing Iliff as a freestanding seminary with its own board of governance, the school was free to move forward. Conflict and controversy were the prologue to progress. "Behold the turtle: it only makes progress when it sticks its neck out!"

In 1919, conflict and controversy once again emerged in the headlines of the press. *The Rocky Mountain News* published a report from the Denver Presbytery stating that Presbyterian students should not go to either the University of Denver or Iliff. Graduates from either school would not be welcome in the Denver Presbytery because both schools were accused of denying the deity of Christ, doubting the authority of Scripture, and teaching "advanced theories" of evolution.

Subsequent investigation showed that no Presbyterian official had visited Iliff before issuing their report and that two of the Presbyterians on the committee who issued the report had sons enrolled at the University of Denver before, during, and after the controversy. The administrations and Trustees of both Iliff and the University of Denver responded by defending the right of both the faculty and the students to explore new theories and to hold beliefs that might not be shared by the majority of the Christian world. This response prompted some local church groups to castigate both schools as "hot-beds of infidelity." Much support also came to the schools. A Presbyterian lawyer wrote:

> The gist of the attack . . . simply is that you have shed the light of modern scientific and historical knowledge and research upon our tenets of religion. . . . I am no Methodist, I am a Presbyterian, . . . but I do appreciate the fact that my church has leveled the true charge against you, of being a dispenser of the light of knowledge. Please do not hesitate to admit it.

From its beginnings in 1892, The Iliff School of Theology has unconditionally locked its doors open . . . open to new truth, open to all backgrounds, open to differing perspectives, open to the

Beyond. To quote from a statement of educational purposes adopted by the Trustees, faculty and administration in 1977, the liberal spirit of Iliff has meant "an openness to new knowledge and truth, a readiness to reexamine old axioms, and a willingness to engage in such theological reformulations as are evoked by new knowledge and experience."[13] The school has always lived on the cutting edge of theological education.

In more recent years conflict and controversy have also emerged. In 1989 Iliff discovered itself in a new whirlwind of publicized conflict and controversy. Two Hispanic members of the faculty—Dr. José Cabezón in philosophy of religion and Dr. Mortimer Arias in evangelism—prompted headlines locally and nationwide. Cabezón was attacked because he was Buddhist and Arias because he had spoken favorably of Latin American liberation theology. Though critics focused on Iliff, the real attack was basically on The United Methodist Church—its historic standards, expectations, and commitments. Just as the Southern Baptist Convention has been split by battles between ultraconservatives and moderates, resulting in their seminaries being discredited and split, there are those within United Methodism who are pressing to undermine and disrupt its theological schools.

In many ways it was a new kind of McCarthyism—only this time in the church. No attempt was made in a right-wing church publication to bring balance, accuracy, or fairness. The author employed innuendos, half-truths, and deliberate distortions. Both Dr. Cabezón and Dr. Arias were victims of character assassination, without even the appearance of due process. Inaccurate statements were made about both men and wild charges were made about Iliff "killing" the region's churches. The United Methodist University Senate was called to investigate Iliff, but simultaneously the University Senate was discredited by the same publication as being composed of ineffectual educators. Even the General Conference of The United Methodist Church was castigated as being too weak.

Our stance at the time was that Iliff would welcome any investigation that official church agencies would want to make. We clearly were upholding the historic standards of the church in every respect. The Commission on Theological Schools of United

Methodism insists on academic freedom in all seminaries that train United Methodist clergy. The Commission on Christian Unity and Interreligious Concerns encourages ecumenical involvement and interreligious understanding and dialogue. We submit extensive yearly reports to the Board of Higher Education and Ministry which outline how we teach United Methodist history, doctrine, and policy, and how we uphold the standards of excellence required for funding through the Ministerial Education Fund. Every year we receive 100 percent funding for the category that measures involvement in service to the church. We have been in the forefront of responding to the church's request that our seminaries be more inclusive of women and racial/ethnic persons. By any test, Iliff meets and exceeds the high standards set forth by United Methodists.

Iliff's new appointments did not break new ground in United Methodist theological education. The appointment of a teacher from another major religious faith to a seminary faculty was hardly unprecedented. The best United Methodist schools have always encouraged an interreligious presence and dialogue. Jewish, Hindu, and Buddhist professors have held tenured professorships at other United Methodist seminaries in the past. The denomination has been in the forefront of encouraging interreligious understanding, even establishing the Commission on Christian Unity and Interreligious Concerns. Rather than labeling Iliff the "liberal bastion" of United Methodist seminaries, it might more accurately be accused of being too slow and conservative historically in recognizing the need and value of greater inclusiveness.

Reasonable Christian persons of good conscience might differ about the wisdom of appointing non-Christians to a seminary faculty, but that certainly doesn't justify unchristian responses that distort the truth or defame another's faith. Such reaction, E. Stanley Jones told us, kept Mahatma Gandhi from becoming a Christian. Gandhi was deeply influenced by Jesus Christ but the intolerance and racism of his followers kept Gandhi from becoming a Christian.

The vicious attack on Dr. Mortimer Arias could not be explained by the assertion that he was influenced by liberation theology.

Other United Methodist seminaries have distinguished liberation theologians on their faculties. Nothing in his writings, sermons, or speeches was cited to justify discrediting this former bishop of the Methodist Church in Bolivia, who was imprisoned for his courageous faith and witness. His academic credentials were sterling; his five books on evangelism and mission are highly acclaimed. His Manifesto on Evangelism has been translated into Chinese and many other languages and is used by Christians around the globe.

Conflict and controversy regarding Dr. Cabezón and Dr. Arias may have been based more on opposition to inclusiveness than on stated factors. Racism may indeed have been the reason for this venom. Overall, the appointments proved to be incredibly valuable to the educational process at Iliff, moving the seminary forward to a more inclusive community, enhancing its academic reputation, increasing its spiritual depth, and expanding its service to the church. Truly, like the turtle, the school made progress only by sticking its neck out!

Explanation, Exposure, and Forgiveness

The purpose of reviewing the case study of one seminary is to remind the reader that conflict and controversy are endemic to dynamic theological schools. Theological education can indeed be a subversive activity, in the best tradition of the biblical prophets. Many other seminaries have experienced similar strife over the decades. They have not only survived but thrived when they have fearlessly faced their opponents and incarnated the gospel of Christ's love in their own work and witness.

A famous United Methodist bishop, G. Bromley Oxnam, wrote a powerful book in 1954, entitled *I Protest,* which responded to the attack he and other Protestant leaders had experienced from the House Committee on Un-American Activities. Often I have returned to what he said on that occasion as I have witnessed scurrilous attacks on the church and seminaries. Current unwarranted attacks being published and spoken fit the religious critics of his time, of which he wrote:

Is there any hatred more damaging to the soul than that of one who claims to speak for a God of love but who, because of inner frustrations and unrealized ambitions, lives in a constant inferiority complex, seeking the publicity satisfaction of attacking others, searing his soul with envy, and coming at last to the place where he repudiates Christ's command, and in desperation cries out, "Thou shalt hate thy neighbor as thyself"? The publications and preaching of this little group are filled with venom. Most hatred for others begins as self-hatred. There is nothing to do but to forgive such persons. Nonetheless, there is an obligation to explain them and to expose them.[14]

Explanation, exposure, and forgiveness are the only recourse for theological educators. If a seminary dares to decide to live on the critical and creative edge of theological education, identifying with the excluded, the poor, and the marginalized of our societies, we must be prepared to experience the sharp and jagged cuts of those who are fearful of the future and dedicated to different visions. We must hear reasoned and legitimate criticisms, seeking to explain our actions and making changes when we are wrong. But we must never be intimidated by those who would undermine our mainline Protestant churches and undercut our theological schools.

CHAPTER FIVE

The Seminary as a Redemptive Community

"Which commandment is the first of all?" Jesus answered, "The first is, 'Hear, O Israel: the Lord our God, the Lord is one; you shall love the Lord your God with all your heart, and with all your soul, and with all your mind, and with all your strength.' The second is this, 'You shall love your neighbor as yourself.'"

MARK 12:28-31

Recent Hollywood movies have been examining various professions. *What About Bob?* profiled in comedy the life of a psychiatrist, *Regarding Henry* charted the transformation of a lawyer after a life-changing injury, and *The Doctor* challenged the medical profession to look at themselves through the eyes of their patients. Now it is only a matter of time before seminary faculty are featured in a full-length Hollywood extravaganza!

In *What About Bob?* Richard Dreyfuss, the psychiatrist, discovered he could not simply give his best-selling "how to" "Baby Steps" book to his client, Bill Murray. He wanted personal attention and care. In *Regarding Henry,* Harrison Ford was portrayed as a ruthless and insensitive lawyer who suddenly and drastically changed when he was shot during a neighborhood robbery. In the difficult journey back to health, he relearned what it meant to care for people, including his wife, child, and clients. In *The Doctor,* William Hurt chastised his medical students early in the film that what their patients needed was competence, not care, for the latter takes too much time. But after he himself experienced the threat of cancer and underwent the impersonality of the medical system, he discovered caring was integral to competence and ordered his medical students into hospital beds for five days to experience bedpans, endless testing, and so on.

Now let the cameras roll and imagine what the next Oscar-winning motion picture will be like when *The Seminary Professor* starts to gross millions at our neighborhood theaters! Just imagine your favorite female professor played by Julia Roberts and some male faculty member portrayed by Tom Cruise! Rumors are that the exact plot has not been chosen, but you can count on Hollywood adding some sex and scandal to enliven this spiritual saga.

One scenario envisions how an academically oriented seminary professor, who specializes in critical analysis, abstract thinking, and sarcastic comments about the church is confronted by an existential personal crisis and experiences a type of conversion. Instead of just handing out her book and pouring knowledge out of her metaphorical pitcher, she becomes actively engaged with students and others on their spiritual journey.

Another possible plot features a professor who realizes it is time to leave the "sacred mountain" of academia, since he hasn't written or published anything for years or made any intellectual contributions to the field. What he does best is caring for people, and he accepts a challenging missionary responsibility. Better yet would be a full-length feature of a faculty member who both publishes books and demonstrates what it means to be in mission and ministry.

Nobody Cares How Much You Know

Whatever the ultimate story chosen by the filmmakers, the basic theme will parallel the sign posted on the door of a seminary faculty member: "Nobody cares how much you know until they know how much you care." I don't know whether that bumper sticker slogan was tacked up by a sensitive professor or whether it represented guerrilla graffiti by disgruntled students. My temptation is to argue with the logic and language of the statement. Graduate education represents the transmission of critical knowledge, not expressions of warm, cuddly feelings. Many great scholarly faculty in the past were never known for their interpersonal charm. Students sought to study with them because of their reputations for intellectual scholarship and knowledge. Seminary faculty members should be selected not for their pastoral qualities but for the keenness of their critical intellectual ability and the promise of their substantial contributions to their disciplines.

But the slogan can't be so easily dismissed. Whether it is applied to seminary faculty or parish pastors, this perplexing truth troubles my conscience. Neither new students nor potential parishioners are particularly impressed by our résumés, by our published books and articles, or by the so-called "eminent" positions and committees we hold in academia or the church. Persons in the '90s question the value and validity of knowledge separated from caring. They want to experience the integrity of professors who believe what they teach and pastors who practice what they preach; persons who act on their convictions, and who live lives of faith and compassion.[1] Their theme song repeats the verse that "nobody cares how much you know until they know how much you care."

Jesus in an Academic Setting

Recall for a moment the familiar story of Jesus arguing with the Pharisees, Sadducees, and the lawyers in the temple. Tom Trotter has said it may be "the only episode in scripture that might be considered an academic setting."[2] Jesus was being questioned by persons of diverse theological and political opinions. Basically they were not the kinds of questions, however, meant to elicit new knowledge, but rather the types of questions meant to entrap or embarrass. A game of academic "one-upmanship" was being played. Tom Trotter noted that

> the Sadducee wanted to know about the Levirate law, whose wife would a woman widowed seven times be in heaven? The Pharisee wanted to know about paying taxes to Caesar. And finally, a lawyer asked, "What is the summary of the law?" As if, on the way from the classroom to the drinking fountain, the professor could wrap up in a few choice sentences the whole range of human thought and aspiration.

Jesus' response to each query was ironic—a useful response in a hostile environment. But to the last question, he answered the familiar summary of the law from Deuteronomy 6, the *Shema Yisroel.* "You know the law. Love the Lord your God with all of your heart, and your soul and your strength." So much for the familiar! But, in Mark, the text suggests that Jesus added a phrase, "Love God with your mind." To his hearers, this liberty with the most familiar text in Israel must have caught their attention. The story suggests, "No one dared ask him any more questions."[3]

As seminary professors, pastors, and other religious teachers and leaders struggle with their calling, this Great Commandment set forth by Jesus provides key criteria for measuring commitment: "Love the Lord thy God with all thy heart, soul, mind and strength, and your neighbor as yourself." Knowing and caring are not two disparate activities but integral dimensions of who we are and what we seek to do.

What a privilege for seminary faculty and administrators to be a part of an intellectual community committed to loving God with our minds. Few people have such an opportunity to devote their lives to study, research, scholarship, teaching, and publication. What a tragedy when persons fail to devote themselves to the pursuit of truth and the search for new knowledge. What a travesty when persons accept the opportunities afforded by tenure and academic freedom, but do not discipline themselves to advance the boundaries of knowledge, to be the most dynamic and creative teachers possible, or to communicate their knowledge to others by writing and publishing. What a temptation to believe that simply by caring for students and others we have fulfilled our calling, when in fact we have not truly fulfilled what it means to love God with our minds.

Our constant challenge is to make our scholarship an altar of worship before God. Academia is not some secular enterprise in contrast to church, but the forum for faculty to critically check out ideas, perceptions, and research. To fully love God with our minds is to face the academic community and receive the criticisms and insights others can and do provide us.

But knowledge in the theological schools is seldom just knowledge for knowledge's sake. Seminaries really do not need disembodied academics who are unrelated to students and the church that makes our existence possible. More conservative and evangelical seminaries have often succeeded at precisely the point where more open and liberal mainstream theological schools have failed. Because they have demonstrated a greater caring involvement with students and churches, they have gained greater support for their work and their ideas. Students want and need to see faculty not only in the forefront of scholarship in the classroom, but also in the chapel worshiping and struggling with our faith.

Incarnating the Gospel

How, as faculty or pastors, do we relate our knowledge to our caring? Many of us I fear know the language of liberation, for example, but are not ourselves liberators. We use God language but we don't know the intimacy of relationship with God. We proclaim a message for the world, but we are isolated from that world and are not personally involved in the mission and ministry of God's people in the world. We attend a lot of conferences and meetings, but we are "convention Christians," since we are never on the front lines caring for the hungry, helping the homeless, visiting the prisoners, or helping the addicted. Christian seminary faculty, like the Christian pastor, are expected to incarnate the gospel, not simply teach or preach about it.

Almost all faculty are deeply involved in the church, not only as speakers and resource leaders, but as active congregational participants. They don't "wear their religion on their sleeves," so sometimes students and others don't realize the depth of their commitment and involvement. Likewise, many faculty are involved in the world, providing direct care to the oppressed and imprisoned, but often they hesitate to share reports of their experiences in the classroom. Seminary students, however, need to be exposed to this personal sense of mission and ministry, so they can experience what it means to love God and neighbor not only with their minds but also with hearts, souls, and strength.

A Kinder, Gentler Church

When George Bush was inaugurated President of the United States, he sketched a vision of how he hoped we could "make kinder the face of the nation and gentler the face of the world." In his revisioning of America he moved away from President Reagan's macho, militaristic models to talk about a country with "unity, diversity, and generosity." He spoke of patriotism in terms of caring for one's neighbor, promoting peace, and increasing tolerance. Bush's presidency often failed to remember and enact this vision, but the dream dare not be discarded.

Both the church and society need to become kinder and gentler. The calling of theological schools is to assist in this process by helping to revision Christian mission and ministry—lay, ordained, and diaconal—that it can become more caring and compassionate, more personal and social, more inclusive and global, more daring and dynamic. President Bush's words are strikingly similar to what United States Senator Robert F. Kennedy spoke in the streets of Indianapolis the night that Martin Luther King, Jr. was assassinated:

> What we need . . . is not division; . . . not hatred; . . . not violence or lawlessness, but love and wisdom, and compassion toward one another, and the feeling of justice toward those who still suffer. . . .
>
> Let us dedicate ourselves to what the Greeks wrote so many years ago: "to tame the savageness of man, make gentle the life of this world."[4]

Metaphors have a power beyond themselves—images shape and influence how we think and act. The way we envision our church and ministry has a profound impact on who we are and what we feel called to be and to do. The value of exploring contemporary images of Christian ministry lies not in particular labels or titles but in the possibility that by revisioning the church's mission and ministry it may have a new identity and vitality. The church, understanding itself as a global ministering community, could do much to "tame the savageness" and "make gentle the life of this world."[5]

A Redemptive Community of Scholars and Students

One image or vision of a theological school is as a redemptive community of scholars and students.[6] Seminaries as redemptive communities should seek to live out Christian faith commitments in their own lives, as well as to prepare leaders for proclamatory, sacramental, and caring activities which have always been central to the ecclesial community. The task of the theological school is to critically and creatively search for truth while at the same time incarnating the heart of the gospel in the way it teaches, counsels, and operates.

I dream of the day when the church truly becomes a redemptive, inclusive community—a kinder, gentler community of faith and love. While the theological school is distinct from the church, yet it has a special responsibility to reflect like a mirror the experience of persons who live in redemptively caring and compassionate ways.

Roman Catholic theologian Henri J. M. Nouwen suggests in his provocative book *Gracias!* that if we are to live and act in the name of Christ then "what I have to offer to others is not my intelligence, skill, power, influence, or connections, but my own human brokenness through which the love of God can manifest itself." The celebrant in Leonard Bernstein's *Mass* says: "Glass shines brighter when it's broken." This, to me, exemplifies the meaning of mission and ministry. "Ministry is entering with our human brokenness into communion with others and speaking a word of hope."[7]

In our contemporary era, as we look toward the church's third millennium, I am persuaded that what the world needs most is to see the possibilities of redemptive relationships. There is a hunger to be touched by persons who not only believe but who also act out of a commitment of unconditional love and acceptance. "Grace" must come off our theological bookshelves and become visible in the ways we live out our existence.

Unfortunately, this spirit of grace and redemption is in short supply not only in our world but also within the church and seminaries. Self-righteousness, moralistic judgment, and hardness of the heart too often are manifested when persons most need an understanding friend, a supportive colleague, a humane policy, or a compassionate response. Amid human brokenness, we too often join those who would trample rather than those who would seek to transform.

Taylor Branch, in his award-winning book *Parting the Waters: America in the King Years 1954-63,* has suggested Martin Luther King, Jr. and the civil rights movement have been the dominant metaphors or symbols of recent decades.[8] In this struggle against racism, the church, despite its failures, has a remarkable record of leadership and compassion. The church today continues to wage battles for inclusiveness and justice.

Now the AIDS (Acquired Immune Deficiency Syndrome) crisis may be the new metaphor or symbol of our time. As of 1993, the World Health Organization estimated between fifteen and twenty-three million people have been infected with the Human Immunodeficiency Virus (HIV), the virus believed to cause AIDS. By the year 2000 it is estimated that the HIV/AIDS epidemic will include 1 of every 100 people on earth.[9] Faced with this major global health threat, the church in general has found itself unable and unwilling to respond. Centuries of homophobic attitudes and behaviors have kept the church far from the front lines of compassion and service. Unless we soon revision our Christian understandings of ministry, we will have failed God and humanity at a most critical moment in history. Martin E. Marty, however, says there is hope. Marty predicts that

> when every tenth fundamentalist preacher's son, every tenth evangelist's offspring, every tenth Pentecostal's child, every 30th priest falls to non-intravenously occasioned AIDS, the church will turn. It turns slowly and tardily, but when it turns, I have hopes for it. Already some fundamentalists, evangelicals, Pentecostals and Catholics are coming up with new theologies and ethics of care. And with hospices and agencies and policies. Do not underestimate the potential of the church when it brings together code and care, Leviticus and love, inherited attitudes and fresh understandings of need, awareness of both God's judgments and steadfast love.[10]

But how long, O God, how long will it be before we revision our ministry and mission so that we can be a kinder and gentler people, a redemptive community?

Revisioning Christian ministry, Roman Catholic scholar Avery Dulles insists, must "be something more than a reflection of the contemporary *Zeitgeist* (spirit of the times)."[11] The biblical and theological roots of ministry and the special mission of the church must be normative. The church will become a more caring and compassionate community, not by the pressure of the contemporary *Zeitgeist,* but as we explore the biblical and theological roots of our ministry and embody the special mission of the church.

Confronted by the enormity of human suffering in this world, the vast numbers of hungry, helpless, and hurting around this globe, we may be tempted to despair. Often we think what little each of us can do in our small place of ministry is not enough and hardly worth doing. How can I do anything in the face of the magnitude of human suffering? But then we need to return to our sacred traditions and listen to the teaching of the ancient sages.

Where, the Jews asked, shall we look for the Messiah? Shall he come to us on clouds of glory, robed in majesty and crowned with light? The Talmud (b. Sanh. 98a) reports that R. Joshua b. Levi put this question to no less an authority than the prophet Elijah himself.

"Where," R. Joshua asked, "shall I find the Messiah?"
"At the gate of the city," Elijah replied.
"How shall I recognize him?"
"He sits among the lepers."
"Among the lepers!" cried R. Joshua. "What is he doing there?"
"He changes their bandages," Elijah answered, "He changes them one by one."

A rabbi says "That may not seem like much for a Messiah to be doing. But apparently, in the eyes of God, it is a mighty thing indeed."[12] Those of us who claim the name of Jesus the Christ dare do no less.

Revisioning Seminary Curriculums

Likewise, new images and metaphors need to be tested in seminary curriculums if theological schools are effectively to prepare persons for Christian ministry and serve as centers for the intellectual life of the church in the twenty-first century. Efforts to combine knowing and caring, the theoretical and the practical, a kinder and gentler church, and redemptive images require various models to be explored.

Unfortunately, when it comes to curriculums, sometimes it proves easier to move a cemetery than change a seminary! Over the years, many a design seeking to reform Master of Divinity programs has been wrecked on the rocks of parochial disciplinary resistance. Churches tend to demand more and more requirements at the same time students are protesting too many requirements. Financial resources remain extremely limited for testing new methodologies and pedagogies. "Fiscal anxieties," reports Donald W. Shriver, past president of Union Theological Seminary in New York, "have had the unfortunate, inevitable consequence . . . of cutting the nerve of much educational planning on the part of both the board and the faculty. Who can plan for a future that is not likely to come?"[13]

One illustration of curriculum reform that I know well occurred at The Iliff School of Theology. The faculty sought to revision the master's degree curriculum in two significant ways. First, a special concentration was developed in the master's program in the area of justice and peace. Students are offered a curriculum tailored to this special missional concern of the church for justice, peace, and the integrity of creation. Second, a new vision of Master of Divinity studies was developed, which attempts to move beyond the current individualistic model of preparing persons for a professional ministry to a more public ministry in a global village. The core requirements, generally team-taught, place increased emphasis on Christian historical, biblical, and theological studies, along with cross-cultural studies, and the cross-disciplinary integration of materials. Field education requirements are incorporated into an expanded program of personal and professional formation. In redesigning the curriculum the faculty stressed the role of religions in a changing world, Christianity in historical perspectives, scripture and interpretation, theology and moral practice, and the church and its mission and ministry.

Education for Christian ministry moves beyond the concept of "professionalism," important as that is, to a recovery of a theological understanding rooted in the essence of the faith, not simply in the mechanics of ministry. In this curriculum revision, Christian ministry is understood within a broad religious context. Perspectives are not only denominational, but also ecumenical and interreligious, helping persons to understand Christian faith and practice amid a world of Hindus, Buddhists, Muslims, and persons of no faith. As M. Thomas Thangaraj has argued:

> How do we ever understand the Bible (which is the book of the story of the oppressed and their liberation) without reading it in the company of the poor and the marginalized? Is it possible at all to come to grips with the history of the Christian Church without a conscious expression of solidarity with the women, and the Afro-Americans in our communities? How can we even dream of understanding world religions if we do not express our solidarity with the people of other faiths in their worship, community life, and their festivals?[14]

The goal is not to diminish the significance of a pastor in the pulpit or a Christian educator in the church school, but to help that person understand the broader contexts in which they serve. Sometimes we think of ourselves as being in isolated, forgotten places, far from the dynamic centers of ministry and mission. In truth, however, if we are in caring ministry to others and striving for justice and peace, then wherever we serve is at the heart of God's action in the world.

For example, when John V. Leach graduated from seminary in 1932, he chose a ministry in rural South Dakota. By academic or even professional standards, he might have thought he was being assigned to an isolated or forgotten place. In 1959, when he traveled to the Holy Land, he could have focused only on the biblical sites. Instead he got involved with a refugee Palestinian mother and her two sons, helping them come to the United States for church-related college educations. The consequence of his vision was that the oldest, Bishara, has established a Christian Bible College in the heart of Bethlehem. The youngest, Mubarek Awad, became an activist and spokesperson for peace and nonviolence in the Palestinian conflict. This Christian witness was viewed as so threatening and subversive by Israeli authorities in the 1980s that he was expelled from his own country. But because as pastor and college professor Leach had a visionary ministry and a deep commitment to justice and peace wherever he was, he helped to lay the framework for the emerging new era in the Middle East. Yes, wherever we serve is at the heart of God's action in the world.

Living Out Our Callings

Merely changing curriculums will not suffice in creating seminaries that are redemptive communities of faith, learning, and hope. Intentional administrative and trustee policies will need to reflect this commitment to humane and caring procedures. Chapel life will need to reinforce this spiritual emphasis. Knowing and caring will need to be connected in the ways students and scholars interact in the classroom, offices, and school activities. Deliberate attempts at developing new partnerships and relationships with vibrant church communities of faith will be essential. In the next chapter, possible ways of accenting both the academic and ecclesiastical will be explored.

Hollywood probably will never produce *The Seminary Professor* for fear that box office receipts won't match those of *The Terminator II* or *Jurassic Park*. The public spotlights are unlikely to lift our faculty professions from obscurity to fame. Unfortunately, Julia Roberts and Tom Cruise may never be seen teaching Bible or theology. Thus, in their own quiet and faithful ways, seminary faculty will have to "star" by living out their calling in the classrooms, balancing knowing and caring, seeking to serve students and the church by loving God with all their heart, soul, strength, and mind.

CHAPTER SIX

Publish *and* Parish

··

In the beginning was the Word, and the Word was with God, and the Word was God. And the Word became flesh and lived among us, . . . full of grace and truth.

JOHN 1:1, 14

P ublish or perish" certainly must be one of the most common clichés recited in contemporary higher education. Like "don't throw the baby out with the bath water" and "practice what you preach," "publish or perish" may be quoted too often, but its truth is not undiminished by excessive repetition. Thoughtful, reflective communities, dedicated to the search for truth and new insights, must be committed to scholarly inquiry where the results are publicly shared and reviewed by peers through an editorial and publication process.

"Publish or perish" language often has been criticized as being too academic or not concerned enough with good teaching. Seminary faculty are criticized for too often writing articles that have a narrow or esoteric audience. Scholars speak to scholars but not to the church or broader community. Allegations are launched, complaining that scholarly writing detracts from time spent in developing good pedagogy. Rather than debate those questions, however, I want to focus on an even more controversial idea germane to the future of theological education: "publish *and* parish."

Confusion can easily occur. Years ago when I was a seminary student in Boston and attempting by letter and telephone to court my fiancée, Bonnie, who was studying in Iowa, we had an interesting experience in communications. At the time I was thinking of returning to India as a missionary. She had expressed some openness to the idea, but then I got a letter from her one day which inadvertently revealed to me her unspoken feelings about possible missionary life. She asked me: "if you go to India, will it be a perish situation?" Instead of spelling it "p-a-r-i-s-h," she wrote "p-e-r-i-s-h"! We laughed about the error, but I decided that if I wanted a happy marriage, God must be calling us to a congregation in our home state of South Dakota! (Parenthetically, I probably should report that my more sophisticated student friends and faculty at Boston and Harvard were convinced that by choosing South Dakota my life and career were indeed doomed to perish!)

This chapter is an invitation to explore what a new model or paradigm like "publish and parish" might mean both to seminary faculty and graduates of theological schools. Outlined will be a few of the possible consequences and benefits that might arise from such a new paradigm, emphasizing both publish and parish.

A Bifocal Vision for Faculty and Administrators

For those of us who teach or administrate in theological schools, the challenge to emphasize both publish and parish will indeed push us in directions many of us will resist. We are more comfortable with the old academic models. While some of us may wish to diminish the publishing pressures, we certainly are not anxious to underscore increased parish involvements for ourselves. Some may actually believe they can be effective teachers and thinkers even if they lack vital relationships and commitments to vital congregations of faith. A few may even want to replace scholarly research and publication with intensive pastoral or lay involvement.

On the horizon, however, I envision not an "either/or" choice, but the imperative of finding a better balance between scholarship and service, theoretical and practical, academic and church life. Teaching that dwells in the realm of theories and esoteric examples, but fails to touch the tender points of reality being experienced by pastors and congregations in today's world, can ultimately prove worthless. If theological schools are to continue their historic commitment to preparing persons for Christian parish ministry, then they must have faculty and administrators who themselves demonstrate a lively awareness of the faith issues and life dilemmas that beset persons both in the pews and pulpits. Effective theological educators simultaneously must have their hearts and minds and souls embedded in the two worlds of church and academia.

Such a bifocal vision should not only make teaching more relevant, but hopefully make publishing more creative, thoughtful, and useful. Clearly there is a need and value for scholars to speak to scholars, but too often that discussion never escapes from that limited circle, and pressing questions of faith, justice, and peace are never addressed. Fortunately, on occasion these publishing patterns are broken. For example, theologian Gordon Kaufman used the occasion of his presidential address at the American Academy of Religion to speak to the dangers of a nuclear holocaust. Likewise, United Methodist theologian John B. Cobb, Jr. has focused some of his books on issues of abortion, sexuality, and the environment, as well as writing articles on pressing questions facing the denominational future of United Methodism. While I celebrate and champion the scholarly publications of my own faculty, I repeatedly challenge them to make their voices and visions more readily accessible and usable to laity and clergy through volumes that will help transform the practical issues of parish life and in articles that will grace the pages of publications like *The Christian Century, Christian Ministry, Circuit Rider, Sojourners, The Other Side,* and *Christianity Today.*

Effective theological scholarship necessitates addressing five related communities. First, scholars must be conversant with the larger academic community, meeting professional standards of research and integrating knowledge from other fields into their work. Second, seminary faculty must relate their scholarship to the church, both locally and globally, ever seeking to discover relationships between disciplinary scholarship and church concerns. Third, every scholar-teacher must individually be a specialist in his or her own field, seeking to advance knowledge in the discipline. Fourth, seminary teachers are called to relate their work to the practical concerns of students and parishes, critically reflecting on theory and practice. Fifth, the challenge to theological scholarship is to encourage the formation of leaders for the churches. "Obviously," as Philip S. Keane and Melanie A. May note, "these groups—the academy, the churches, the specialists, the practitioners, and the leaders—can often be in tension with one another. Theological scholarship is a special challenge because of the many and sometimes competing communities that have a stake in the activity of theological scholars."[1]

An Invitation to Pastors and Laity

This invitation of "publish and parish," however, is not only directed to seminary faculty and administrators, but also to all Christian laity and clergy. Research, reflection, and writing are not only requirements of academics, but requisites for all persons in ministry.

Theological educators Joseph C. Hough, Jr. and John B. Cobb, Jr. have advocated that the church of the future requires practical theologians as its ministers. This metaphor combines two images: the practical Christian thinker and the reflective practitioner. Stressing the need for ministers to be visionary pathfinders or problem solvers, Hough and Cobb insist that thinking be oriented to practice and guided by a deep sense of Christian identity. Issues such as global survival and human sexuality need to be addressed by persons who think from the perspective of what it means to be a Christian.

Every follower of Jesus Christ, lay or clergy, is called to be a practical theologian. The obligation is to think, to inquire, to explore, and to ask critical questions. Theologizing is an integral part of being a believer. Tragically, many Christians seem to leave their brains outside the sanctuary and show little interest in relating their faith to their daily activities and political opinions. Some religious practitioners appear to have given leave of their senses. Spirituality has at times been confused with irrationality. As the wall poster reminds us: "Jesus came to take away our sins, not our minds."[2]

Beware of the seduction of thinking you cannot write or publish because you don't have a Ph.D. Reinhold Niebuhr had no advanced degrees beyond his basic seminary training; yet he has had tremendous intellectual, social, church, and political influence. He began writing when he was a parish pastor in Detroit. Though written in 1929, his book, still in print, *Leaves from the Notebook of a Tamed Cynic,* ought to be mandatory reading for every person entering the contemporary parish. Recently when Erik H. Erikson died, I realized for the first time that he never had a college degree, only a standard diploma from a German high school. Though a member of the faculty of Harvard Medical School, he had never studied medicine. Yet his thinking and publications have had an impact on generations of persons seeking to understand the mysteries of human growth and personality development. His books on Martin Luther and Mahatma Gandhi, *Young Man Luther* (1958) and *Gandhi's Truth* (1969), have provided provocative challenges to our theological thinking.

Niebuhr and Erikson, of course, are exceptional, but that should not become an excuse. Not everyone can or should write a book, but thoughtful laypersons and seminary graduates can articulate their faith and vision in timely public letters to editors, columns in church newsletters, articles in religious magazines, communications to secular newspapers, and so on. "Publish and parish" can provide an added dimension to one's ministry, moving one outside the traditional four walls of the sanctuary and into the public realm of discourse and dialogue. It can be a prophetic forum for an evangelistic witness.

Risking Controversy

Venturing forth into public print, however, means risking controversy. More than once my writings have got me into trouble. In high school I wrote a statewide column in a youth fellowship publication that got a lot of attention because I erroneously declared "it was more blessed to receive than to give" (perhaps that reveals why I chose a career in fund-raising). I nearly got thrown out of college as a sophomore because in the student newspaper I challenged the autocratic administration.[3]

Once a Christmas devotional that I wrote got published in the daily newspaper. An ultraconservative Lutheran pastor denounced me as a heretic in a series of letters to the editor. Never have so many persons in that community ever read and debated theology, as people went scrambling through old newspapers! Another article I wrote calling for compassion and understanding upset many self-appointed moralists. Just recently a hurting pastor reminded me of that guest editorial in which I declared that "the church is the only army in the world that shoots its wounded soldiers."

Strange as it may seem, at least one of the sharpest critics of United Methodist theological education has been "used" by the Unification Church. The "Moonies" have sponsored lavish "academic" conferences and paid scholars' expenses to participate, flying them to South Korea, Hawaii, and other resort places. In contrast, I have been attacked as narrow-minded because of my outspoken opposition to their movement. A movie review I published about cults and brainwashing in *The Christian Century* so irritated the Unification Church that they accused me "of a deep-rooted religious prejudice and an unfortunate ignorance in a president of a theological seminary."[4]

I believe persons are best known by the enemies they make. Publishing about pastoral matters often helps illuminate one's most profound commitments and concerns and assists us in identifying those forces that stand in opposition. Leadership necessitates persons articulating their deepest concerns and highest visions for the church and society.

Richard J. Mouw, president of Fuller Theological Seminary, reminds seminary faculty of the necessity of challenging the hegemony of the academic guilds in the realm of seminary teaching and scholarship. "My sense," says Mouw, "is that while seminary scholars have paid much more attention to the need to speak *to* the church and *to* the public square we have thought little about how to speak *to* the academy. We have been more intimidated by the academic guilds than we have by our other two publics."[5] Theological scholarship must risk the controversy of confronting the dominance of academia.

Yes, I would acknowledge there is a danger in publish *and* parish, since once we move outside the comfortable confines of current scholarship and dare to speak in various settings, we risk conflict and controversy. But by embracing both publish and parish, we also may discover new possibilities for expressing our Christian faith, as we merge theory and practice, thought and life, critical thinking and caring compassion. All of us—faculty, administrators, laity, and clergy—are called to be reflective practitioners. Perhaps by making publish *and* parish our personal and professional goal, we will not only discover new levels of self-fulfillment but also enrich the church and academia that we love.

Is It Word Processing or Processing the Word?

As we move toward a new era that includes the information superhighway, computers are increasingly becoming one of the most valuable tools a minister can have, particularly if one adopts the "publish *and* parish" model. Over the years, the mechanics of ministry have pushed us from horses to cars, from mimeograph machines to photostat equipment, from the pony express to electronic mail, from typewriters to computers, and from taping together manuscripts to word processing.

At each step of rapid change, some people have decided to resist change. One generation refused to learn to use electric typewriters; now another says that they can get along without computers. Sometimes when trying to adapt to new methodologies or equipment, one feels the frustration is not worth the effort. What happened at St. Mark's Lutheran Church in Victoria, Australia, is illustrative. Producing a funeral bulletin for a woman named Edna, the church secretary decided just to use the search-and-replace key to amend the bulletin from the previous funeral for a woman named Mary. Every time Mary's name appeared, the computer inserted Edna. Imagine the consternation of mourners when they began to recite the Apostles' Creed, and read that Christ "was conceived by the Holy Spirit and born of the Virgin Edna."[6]

How can I ever forget, for example, my first harrowing experience when I was learning the technique of word processing? My initial attempt to type a Christmas sermon to deliver to area pastors and spouses went very well until I attempted to have it printed. At that point, I discovered that I didn't know how to make the printer work. Instead of having a nicely typed manuscript, have you ever tried to preach from a floppy disk? Oh, how I wished that I had learned the method of manuscriptless preaching! Reflecting on this experience, along with observing the rapidly computerized world of church and seminary, has prompted me to ponder whether we are engaged in theological education for the primary purpose of "word processing" or "processing the Word".

The use of the term *word* in Christian theology and history is so rich and extensive that with only a cursory glance it can be noted. Protestantism, in particular, has strongly emphasized "theologies of the Word" and "proclamation of the Word." *Word* in the Hebrew Bible usually means a spoken utterance of any kind, a saying, speech, or message. Some Old Testament books are a collection of written sayings: "The words of Amos" or Jeremiah, or Ecclesiastes. Other times *word* in the Old Testament refers to an event or act. Nearly 400 times the phrase "the word of the Lord" appears, referring to an act of communication from the divine to the human.

Likewise, in the New Testament there are variations in the use of the term we translate in English as *word.* Especially dominant is the term *logos,* which cannot be translated by any single term in English. Borrowed from the Stoics, it was far more than spoken language; it was what gave order and shape to the process of thinking. It was almost equivalent to *rationality* for the Greeks, but for the Jews it had connotations of how God communicated with humans. For some the images of *wisdom* seemed apparent. Jesus the Christ was proclaimed the Logos, the Word of God.

When Christians think about *Word,* the passage of Scripture most quickly recalled is drawn from the prologue of the Gospel of

John. Instead of beginning the Gospel with humble Lukan stories of mangers and shepherds, or starting even like Matthew with kings and sages, John rolls the drums of philosophy and blows the trumpets of theology. Like the crescendo sound of a great orchestra, the writer of John captures in lofty language an overture that transcends monotone prose in favor of majestic poetry:

> In the beginning was the Word, and the Word was with God, and the Word was God. (John 1:1)

> And the Word became flesh and lived among us, . . . full of grace and truth. (John 1:14)

Beyond Word Processing

Taking some liberty with these two passages, let me suggest something of the possible distinction between "Word processing" and "processing the Word." By dictionary definition, *processing* can mean to treat, prepare, or handle by some special method. For example, there is processing fruit and vegetables for market, processing cloth to make it waterproof, or processing information via a computer. Much of theological education, you might say, is devoted to "Word processing," i.e., treating, preparing, or handling theological materials by special methods and disciplines.

The first text cited from the Gospel of John is magnificent in its abstraction, postulating theories upon theories. "In the beginning was the Word, and the Word was with God, and the Word was God." Consult biblical commentaries and you will discover endless discussion about what these terms meant and what they might mean today. As someone remarked, "Jesus is not to be interpreted by Logos; Logos is intelligible only as we think of Jesus." Rudolph Bultmann declares that "it is precisely the mythological description of Jesus Christ" that makes "clear" how "the figure and the work of Jesus Christ are to be understood as the divine work of redemption."[7] A plethora of paradoxical possibilities abound, ever ripe for theological disputation.

All of which leads me to warn of the danger of a theological school becoming simply a "Word processing" institution, rapidly spewing out abstract theological credos without due regard to the realities toward which words can only point. As Henri J. M. Nouwen has noted:

> Often it seems that we who study or teach theology find ourselves too entangled in such a complex network of discussions, debates and arguments about God and God issues that a simple conversation with God or a simple presence to God has become harder instead of easier. Our heightened verbal ability, which enables us to make many distinctions, has sometimes become a poor substitute for a single-minded commitment to the words "Who is life?"[8]

Lest one think Nouwen belongs to the anti-intellectual camp, perhaps it should be noted that he knows theological communities all too well, having taught at both Harvard and Yale Divinity Schools. Much of his ministry has been devoted to justice and peace issues. He argues that "this is not to say empirical intellectual work and the subtle distinctions it requires have no place in theological training. To the contrary, they are essential to mature ministry. But when our words are no longer a reflection of the divine word in and through which the world has been created and redeemed, they lose their grounding and become a seductive and misleading word."[9]

Processing the Word in Our Own Lives

What Nouwen is hinting at is that we must not forget in our "Word processing" intellectual pursuit that there are other critical dimensions to theological education, namely "processing the Word" in our own lives. The paths of spiritual formation are many, but they most often include cultivating the holy habits of prayer, meditation, and Scripture reading. We too might experience the surprising serendipity of the seminary student, who, while reading the Bible, was overheard exclaiming: "This gives real light on the commentaries!"

Another dictionary definition suggests that *processing* can refer to a course of action or procedure; the idea that we are internalizing what we are saying or proclaiming; or make our deeds match our words.

An abstract God is never enough. A remote theory, however admirable or true, cannot compare with a practical illustration. And so the Gospel writer proclaimed: "And the Word became flesh and lived among us, . . . full of grace and truth." Obviously this passage raises as many questions as answers, and needs the discipline of rigorous theological examination, but it reminds us of the central importance of the Incarnation.

"Grace" and "truth" are understood, not simply by logical discourse or disputation, but when lives become the gospel. Many a person would testify with Matthew Arnold that it was not our parents' teachings but our parents' lives, lived day by day, both positive and negative, that made the difference in our own faith journey. United States President Ronald Reagan would have been more persuasive in his "pro-family" rhetoric, if it hadn't taken him twenty months to arrange to see his grandchild!

The concept of *agape* (love) is made far more persuasive when its exponents demonstrate its reality in the way they treat others. Faculty who forget what students can teach them are hardly exemplars of learning. The idea of justice takes on new meaning when we see its advocates moving beyond lip service. Liberation theologians are more persuasive when their lifestyles reflect their rhetoric. America's claims for wanting peace are more likely to be believed when we restrain from being the policeman of the world and decline to intervene in the affairs of our neighbors.

Quintin Hogg once wrote that he does not care to what denomination a person belongs. He declared, "I do not very much care what special creed you profess, but I do care beyond all expression that the result of that creed in your daily life should be to make you a power for good amongst your fellow human beings." So many persons have perfected their creeds and their theologies, but there is little self-evident in their life and work to attest to their beliefs.

An exception was a friend of mine, Wallie Wahlberg, who, until his recent death, would have characterized himself as an "unreconstructed social gospel liberal," still affirming the "building of the Kingdom of God on earth," as if Reinhold Niebuhr had never written *Moral Man and Immoral Society* more than forty years ago, demonstrating the power of sin and the illusion of bringing the Kingdom to earth.

Yet, if we reflect on "processing the Word," we cannot help being awed by Wahlberg's more than eighty years of committed pastoral service in the interest of the poor, the downtrodden, the oppressed of this world. Throughout his long life he believed the pen was more powerful than the sword, and he wrote letters to editors, articles, and books urging social justice and mercy. His was a ministry of publish *and* parish. In Colorado history he is regarded as one of the most powerful and prophetic Christian voices of this century. Governor Richard Lamm called him the "conscience of Colorado." During the 1930s he transformed his local Denver church into a massive social service agency, organized the unemployed, and was credited with having avoided massive riots among the people. Instead, he gave them new hope and opportunity. Since he believed in the impossible, and made the gospel incarnate in his own life and ministry, Niebuhrian pessimism about the possibilities of love and justice in human group experience did not cut his nerve for Christian social action. By "processing the Word," Wahlberg became what Quintin Hogg triumphed as most essential: "a power for good" among other human beings.

Obviously, I have overstated the dichotomy of choices. For those of us engaged in theological education, it is never a simple choice of *either* "Word processing" or "processing the Word." Both are essential dimensions of our own spiritual development and our life together. Rigorous graduate education, professional training, and spiritual formation are all imperatives if we are to be powers for good in our global village. The disciplined mind and discerning heart are *both* needed, if we are to be holistic persons and winsome ministers of the gospel of Jesus Christ, "full of grace and truth."

CHAPTER SEVEN

Prepare a Superhighway for Our God

"In the wilderness prepare the way of the LORD, make straight in the desert a highway for our God."

ISAIAH 40:3

I n the 1950s, during the presidency of Dwight Eisenhower, the United States launched a major construction effort to build a national interstate highway system. Built originally in the interest of national defense, this network of roads has proved to be a major economic stimulus to the nation, moving goods and people quickly and conveniently anywhere in the country. Now, forty years later, the United States is involved with people around the world to create a new information superhighway, which will transport ideas and knowledge beyond national and cultural barriers. President Bill Clinton has asked Congress to pass legislation to help "connect every classroom, every clinic, every library, every hospital in America into a national information superhighway by the year 2000."

Biblical Images of Highways

Will the church and seminary be left out of this new information superhighway? Will we continue to wander down the old lanes and pathways, while the rest of the world spins messages off satellites and communicates across cyberspace? Or will we give new meaning to the old vision of the prophet Isaiah: "In the wilderness prepare the way of the LORD, make straight in the desert a highway for our God"?

113

The Bible often uses the metaphor of building highways. In Isaiah the reference is to constructing a road through the desert separating Babylon from Palestine, which was impassable because of its lack of water and dangerous slopes. "Highway," in this instance, refers to the exodus-conquest from Egypt to Canaan through the wilderness of Sinai. It is the triumphant victory procession of the people to God's shrine. Israel's triumphant return home demonstrates Yahweh's glory because other nations will see how God can rescue people from Babylon and restore them.[1]

In the parable of the great banquet (Luke 14:15-24), Jesus told a story in which the invited guests are too busy to dine, so the servant is instructed first to "go out at once into the streets and lanes of the town and bring in the poor, the crippled, the blind, and the lame." This symbolizes an invitation to all the people of the land, including those most marginalized by society. But since there continues to be room at the table, the servant is ordered to "go out into the roads and lanes" in order to get guests. This symbolizes God's mission to the wider Gentile world. The messianic banquet in God's kingdom is open to everyone on the globe.

Highways also played an important role in the spread and development of the early Christian church. The Roman Empire was noted for its road making and aqueducts, and the early Christian community capitalized on the network of roads that they created. The evangelistic efforts of the early church took advantage of their new opportunities for travel and communication.

Road Signs on the Superhighway

Now the challenge Christians face at the dawn of the new millennium is whether the contemporary church and seminary will take advantage of the new opportunities awaiting us with the emerging information superhighway. Will it be true that United Methodists don't just ride the circuit, but also plug into it? Or will churches resist the age of cyberfaith? While laypeople, and especially younger generations, eagerly embrace the new technology, the danger is that the church will move not just carefully, but fearfully, into this new communications revolution.

Lest there be any misunderstanding, I am just a hitchhiker or student driver on this new superhighway. During my study leave, I have begun to learn the rules of the road, the location of the entrance ramps, and the language signs posted along the way. Far from being a race car driver, cruising at fantastic speeds around the racetrack of computers, modems, and the Internet, I have just begun to test drive in these exciting new lanes of communication. In doing so, I have learned a few helpful items I probably should share.

First, cyberspace is the space that lies between two telephones, not in the instruments themselves but in the unseen space between, in the area where the conversation takes place. Cyber is a new prefix that is added to words to signify this new world of communicating and relating. Thus, people talk not only about cyberspace, but also about cyberfood and cyberfaith or even cyber Methodists or cyber Muslims! In Dallas, Texas, a High Tech Café recently opened offering computers and modems during lunch, so that "people can download their lunch and their computers at the same time—taking bytes between bites, you might say."[2]

Second, the information superhighway is not quite a reality yet, but it is developing faster than many of us realize. What has come to be called the information superhighway is a crossbreeding of computer networks, cable television, interactive telephones, and whatever other technologies allow us to explore cyberspace. Unlike cyberspace, which is intangible, the highway is composed of tangibles—computers, televisions, modems, phones, fiber-optic cables, and so on. Currently, it is a global web of 30,000 computer networks, at least 2.2 million computers and more than 20 million people in more than 70 countries.

Third, we drive on this information superhighway via the Internet, which is actually a network of computer networks (or a bunch of computers hooked together). No one really runs this Internet system; it is kind of a cooperative in cyberspace. Begun in 1969 by the United States Defense Department, it was created to connect the Pentagon with military research in academia and business. In 1986 the National Science Foundation spurred nondefense use in the United States by connecting five supercomputing centers across the country. Now it has spread to every continent—even Antarctica, the land of penguins, is linked by computers!

Fourth, electronic mail (or E-mail) is the most widely used way people move on the information superhighway, with millions of people around the world communicating with one another. As citizens of cyberspace, people are transcending national, religious, ethnic, cultural, and political barriers. China discovered that despite its efforts at censorship, real news about the Tiananmen Square massacre reached the outside world by fax. During the attempted 1991 Soviet coup, when telephones were cut off and newspapers weren't published, the world kept in touch with Moscow with a tiny Internet provider in Finland called RELCOM. But most of the time, citizens of cyberspace are writing memos to one another, exchanging food recipes, rumors, ideas, and other types of information. Even love letters flow across cyberspace—in America, right-wing talk show host Rush Limbaugh recently married a woman who first contacted him by E-mail! Around the world people now communicate by fax machines, sending messages in seconds rather than using the old postal systems that took days, weeks, and even months.

Recently discovered on the electronic mail communication called Ecunet was an unsolicited testimonial from a graduate of a United Methodist theological seminary:

> I can report that I've been VERY happy with the seminary education I received. . . . I chose to take a year internship even after all my field ed had been finished because I realized I needed a place to make my mistakes, learn from them, and move away from them without them following me into the next church. Great, painful, loving, touching, gut wrenching year with experiences I'll never forget (like falling into the grave under the casket during my first funeral). That internship let me find what I could do as well as what I couldn't do. Fourteen years later I still believe I made the right choice. . . . Fourteen years later I'm ready for more seminary work.

There may be possibilities for public relations and stimulating recruitment via electronic mail that theological schools have not yet imagined. If Rush Limbaugh can find the love of his life, then surely seminaries can find a few good students!

The Information Superhighway as God's Great Gift

Truly, the emerging information superhighway is one of God's great gifts to the new world of the twenty-first century. Therefore, let me invite you to look forward into the future and imagine some of the possibilities that exist along the new information superhighway for enhancing the mission and ministry of Christ's church in the world. Truly, Christians live in a time when many people are living in cultural wildernesses and spiritual deserts. It is precisely in this context that we need to be Isaiahlike voices crying out:

> "In the wilderness prepare the way of the LORD,
> make straight in the desert a highway for our God."

We need to re-echo the language of John the Baptist:

> "Prepare the way of the Lord, . . . and all flesh shall see the salvation of God." (Luke 3:4, 6)

How can the church, its seminaries, and ministry employ the resources of the new information superhighway for the glory of God? How can the mission and ministry be enhanced? Let me briefly suggest five ways, encouraging you to share other ideas and possibilities for mission and ministry.

First, the possibilities of personal and professional theological growth and understanding have been increased by the revolution in computers and cyberspace communications. Church Bytes, a church computer magazine, is now in its tenth year of publication. More than 200 companies now produce software for churches. These products, reports David Gonzales, run "the gamut from the ever-popular Bible study software that allow for comparisons of biblical texts in English, Greek and Hebrew to arcade-quality games, like Defender of the Faith, that add a dose of religion to the usual video shoot-'em-ups."[3]

Just as the Bible was one of the first books to be printed, so it has become available as a computer product. Bible study software, originally intended for ministers and seminarians, is now often used by laypersons wanting to know about the Bible. Logos Resources has developed a Windows-based software program that permits a user to have a half-dozen Bible translations on the screen simultaneously. A concordance is available for looking for Bible words and names. A Bible atlas helps persons graphically see the countries of the Old and New Testaments, as well as explore maps of events like the battle of Jericho or retrace the journeys of Paul. CD-ROM software is being developed that will provide video images and full sound. These materials are being published in English, Korean, Spanish, French, and many other languages.

Continuing education opportunities are arising almost faster than we imagine them. Cost is a major factor for most pastors, but as computers spread and prices are reduced, tremendous possibilities for continued learning are emerging. Sophisticated programs offering speed-of-light word and phrase searches, plus commentary searches, personal study notes, textual criticism, various translations, and more provide wonderful tools for sermon preparation and teaching opportunities. Hopefully these will be time savers, giving persons more time to think and prepare their sermons. But, says Arthur J. Moen, "confronted with hard-disk programs approaching 70 mega-bytes and CD-ROMs [compact disks, read-only memory] with 150,000 pages of information, the pastor may reach overload."[4] The ever present danger of confusing information for knowledge was expressed by T. S. Eliot:

> Where is the Life we have lost in living?
>
> . . . .
> Where is the knowledge we have lost in information?
> The cycles of Heaven in twenty centuries
> Bring us farther from God and nearer to the Dust.[5]
> Choruses from "The Rock"

Improved church administration is a second possibility being offered by computers and cyberspace communications. Specially designed software for church management is flooding the market. It can help spot changing attendance patterns, giving trends, and keep mailing records up-to-date. Noting sudden changes in attendance may signal, for example, a family crisis prompting a pastoral call.

Denominations and their agencies are increasingly using Internet for communications purposes. The Southern Baptist Convention has a network that helps some 2,300 people to keep in touch through electronic messages. It also provides a channel for news within the church and enables them to hold on-line church conferences and programs. Recently, the North American section of the World Methodist Council heard its president speak via satellite television from England and then participants engaged in a question-and-answer session. Ecunet provides an ecumenical communications bulletin board for persons to exchange religious news and engage in extended conversations on theological topics.

Local churches are discovering opportunities for renewal and reformation via the new information superhighway. White's Chapel United Methodist Church in Southlake, Texas, was just about ready to close its doors three years ago. Instead, the new pastor was persuaded by one of the lay members to try computers in his ministry. The layperson, Steve Scott, says "we're all missionaries, we're all disciples. We're really in the communications business creating awareness and visibility for the programs and ministry of the church." So the church began developing mailing lists for brochures announcing new programs, used automated phone calls to thank people for visiting the church, created a database to identify people by interests as well as to keep the pastor updated about important anniversaries and birthdays. Apparently these efforts have proved effective, as 163 new members have joined the church and monthly contributions have climbed from $6,000 to $28,000.[6]

Closely related is a third option: extending the church's ministry of prayer, evangelism, teaching, and even counseling via the new information superhighway. The vision of John the Baptist can take on new meaning when one translates his words into cyberspace:

> "Prepare the way of the Lord,
> make his paths straight.
> Every valley shall be filled,
>   and every mountain and hill shall be made low,
> and the crooked shall be made straight,
>   and the rough ways made smooth;
> and all flesh shall see the salvation of God."
>
> (Luke 3:4-6)

Old barriers can crumble and new ways of sharing the Good News of Jesus Christ can be discovered.

119

Christians around the world are now being linked in computerized prayer networks. Illustrative is Sharon Castellanos, who every week turns on her computer in San Juan, Puerto Rico, and begins to pray. She is not asking for divine help to overcome a balky disk drive or a blank screen, as some of us are tempted to do! No, this is a part of her religious habit of spending an hour of fellowship and prayer with an on-line prayer group. People share prayer requests and exchange spiritual insights via the Internet.[7]

Southern Baptist missionaries are receiving Sunday school materials via electronic mail. United Methodists, Southern Baptists, and others are increasingly communicating with their missionaries by fax machines, satellite phones, and electronic mail. Possibilities for mission and evangelism are expanding as people discover new ways of communicating the gospel.

Christians, however, aren't the only ones surfing the waves of the new communication ocean. Digitized Korans and Buddhist holy books are available. Muslims can use the Internet to access Mas'ood Cajee's Cyber Muslim document, which provides introductory information on Islam, addresses of North American mosques, and the latest information on events in the Islamic world. The scarcity of teachers in Riga, Latvia, doesn't stop yeshiva students from learning about Judaism, thanks to computer links with teachers in Moscow, London, and Israel. Rabbi Yosef Kazen claims that communicating by computer is not as impersonal as it might seem. In fact, he says being faceless has some advantages: "Some guy in a black hat and tefillin comes to you and you have the stereotype. When you go to the Internet and you read about Judaism you go straight to the intellect and the stereotypes fall away. It will unite body and mind. This is not an 18th century guy on the street. It's Judaism in practice."[8]

Religious counseling opportunities also present themselves via the Internet. The newest and highest forms of technology are being used to raise the oldest and deepest questions. People who would never otherwise meet are coming together in cyberspace. Social lives have been transformed as homebound persons are able to communicate. The United Methodist General Board of Global Ministries sponsors a computerized network to aid communication among persons with HIV/AIDS and those who care for them. On-line services provide forums by which people can share their beliefs and exchange religious information. It is often a lay movement, away from the realm of bishops and archbishops. It reduces barriers between religions and increasingly is democratizing religious dialogue both between faiths and within denominations. Tom Sims, who helps moderate Religion Forum on CompuServe reports that "people do talk openly about concerns, so I'm really aware of the diversity of religious belief. I've developed some deep respect for some religious traditions that I didn't have quite as much personal contact with and I've begun to appreciate some of the common threads."[9]

The Possibilities of Cyberseminaries

Cyberseminaries along the information superhighway are a fourth emerging possibility. Until recently limited imaginations and high costs have combined to keep this option from becoming reality, but experiments are now moving forward that provide exciting opportunities.

The Iliff School of Theology, for example, has been exploring various possibilities. It may prove viable to create a church leadership institute in Moscow, Russia, providing theological education by E-mail, as well as by using videotapes, and other media. Potentially this may be a cooperative effort with theological educators in South Korea. Even places as remote and historically isolated from Christianity as Nepal might be served in this way. United Theological Seminary in Dayton, Ohio, will start offering this January a Doctor of Ministry program, which will combine computer technology and ministry to mentally and physically challenged people. In Indiana, faculty at Notre Dame University are teaching theology with the aid of computers. Teaching liturgy, for example, is greatly enhanced by incorporating music as background to specific images projected on a video screen via computer.[10]

The use of satellite television networks provides especially promising opportunities for teaching. Currently it costs about $10,000 for the average hookup, but costs are expected to decrease.

Teleconferencing greatly reduces the cost of bringing participants together, since air travel is quite expensive. In the spring of 1994, a video teleconference on the issue of sexual misconduct by church leaders attracted over 4,000 people at 120 satellite downlink sites in North America. Two experts in the field, Dr. Marie Fortune of Seattle and Dr. Larry Graham of The Iliff School of Theology, spoke during this six hour teleconference, which included time for people all across the country to use a toll-free number to dialogue with the leaders. Entitled "Healing Broken Lives and Communities" it truly was an educational effort that "the crooked shall be made straight, and the rough ways made smooth; and all flesh shall see the salvation of God" (Luke 3:5-6).

Electronic mail has provided the classroom setting for a pioneering effort at Iliff, led by Sally Geis and Sue Calvin. Last spring a regular Iliff class taught by two professors, Dana Wilbanks and Thomas Troeger, was expanded by adding seven persons via E-mail in distant rural places in Utah, Wyoming, and Colorado. Each pastor and professor had a personal computer with access to Ecunet via Bizlink software. An electronic lectionary was created, with clergy preparing sermons and sharing them with the faculty and one another through computer modem connections. "Preaching on Ethical Issues" moved off the campus into cyberspace and into the congregations of people struggling to live out the gospel. Literally, in the great Western wilderness and deserts of the United States, we sought to prepare a highway for our God!

Seminaries will need to create educational centers if they are to be participants with the church on the new information superhighway at Iliff. Why shouldn't seminaries be at the forefront—cyberseminaries serving the church and world in the twenty-first century? Generally, the first steps include computerizing seminary libraries and services, so that not only students on campus, but also pastors and laity can access collections through modems in their studies. Theological school offices have been computerized, and more and more faculty are becoming computer literate. Computer services for students, however, are almost nonexistent. Often even video equipment is minimal and wearing out. Television screens are a rarity in many seminary classrooms. Thanks to a donor's gift, one seminary had a television disk on its roof for years, but only recently was it actually hooked up. The first attempt at continuing education was a disaster, when a large group gathered for a program on preaching, but instead received from satellite a lingerie show! Learning from that lesson, embarrassed seminary officials thereafter made sure that special training was received by operators and that first time programs were done on a very limited experimental basis. Most theological schools are just now beginning to walk on the new information superhighway and to dream and plan for future programming. Opportunities abound for both church and seminary to truly prepare a highway for our God!

Creating a New Global Community

Yet to be fully explored is a fifth dimension—how the information superhighway will help create a new global community. Boundaries and barriers can be leaped in this new age. Fiber-optics helped break up the communist block in Eastern Europe and threatens communism's future in Asia. As people communicate via their modems, they work across all hours, time zones, and geographical borders. The information monopolies of governments, television empires, and newspaper magnates are being broken as millions of people talk directly with millions of others.

The negative side of the information superhighway dare not be ignored. Expect some "roadkill" along the electronic road as well. The predominance of Western culture in regard to television especially undermines spiritual and cultural values in many societies. As television moves into the interactive age, what will be the impact of sex, drugs, and rock and roll on the several hundred million who will be watching music videos on MTV daily from Russia to Guam?[11] A widening gap between the "haves" and the "have-nots" in the information age appears inevitable, as the more affluent have access to computers, the Internet, faxes, and so forth. While the new interactive media will offer new opportunities for spiritual and cultural values, Charles M. Oliver also reminds us that "the same press that Gutenberg used to print his famous Bible was used shortly thereafter to print pornography."[12]

On a more hopeful note, Howard Rheingold in his book *The Virtual Community: Homesteading on the Electronic Frontier* suggests that new kinds of communities are being created as people gather around individual computer screens and begin talking to one another. People are reaching out to one another, just as they did in a former time in small towns and neighborhoods. He tells a poignant story of how parents of an ill child sought help via E-mail, and the kind of practical advice and solace they received. A new type of human connection is becoming possible that transcends race, religion, ethnicity, sexual orientation, age, and nationality. Is the dream of the global village or global neighborhood finally about to arrive? Can the Christian vision of communities without boundaries and borders become a reality?

The new possibilities for communication and information hopefully can enable us as Christians to reach out in love and care toward the whole world. Already we have been able to link resources of food, shelter, and clothing through Church World Service and the United Methodist Committee on Relief, so that our hearts of compassion result in care and action throughout the globe. Korean Methodists and United Methodists work hand in hand, thanks to the new information superhighway, in providing needed relief to persons facing starvation or finding themselves refugees. The new information superhighway hopefully can become a means by which Christians can join in God's liberating and loving mission in the world. Truly, God's great gift of this emerging superhighway can give new meaning to the old vision of the prophet Isaiah:

> "In the wilderness prepare the way of the LORD,
> make straight in the desert a highway for our God."

In Conclusion

The vision of the contemporary church and seminary set forth in this book calls us to join God's mission and ministry in the world. Instead of reminiscing about a nostalgic "not-so-good old days" when theological education was almost exclusively the province and privilege of white Western male clergy, the emerging dream for ministerial education embraces the great diversity of God's peoples as well as the new technological possibilities for communicating the gospel.

Augustine once said that "hope has two beautiful daughters. Their names are anger and courage; anger at the way things are, and the courage to see that they do not remain the way they are."[13] Christians need to go beyond acrimony and anger about what is wrong with our churches and seminaries by demonstrating creativity and courage in envisioning a new future. In the same Augustinian spirit, George Bernard Shaw once declared that "some [people] see things as they are and say why. I dream things that never were and say why not."[14] Visionary theological educators focus not primarily on the issue of *why,* but on the possibilities of *why not.* Therefore, may the children of hope—anger and courage—serve as catalysts for change as we explore new alternatives for the church and seminaries in the years ahead.

Faithfulness to the historic traditions, scripture, theology, and experience of the Christian Church calls us to be pathfinders in the twenty-first century, sharing a vision of what the future of our churches and seminaries should look like, and what values should triumph. Remember the words of Robert Frost, who wrote:

> Two roads diverged in a wood, and I—
> I took the one less traveled by,
> and that has made all the difference.[15]
> "The Road Not Taken"

Our challenge is to reach beyond the past and choose the road "less traveled by," hopefully making "all the difference" in the next millennium.

NOTES

Preface

1. Peter Cartwright, *Autobiography of Peter Cartwright* (Nashville/New York: Abingdon Press, 1956), 64.
2. These words come from the charter of The Iliff School of Theology in Denver, Colorado. Similar phrases and concepts characterize the founding documents of other theological schools.
3. Thomas C. Oden, *Requiem: A Lament in Three Movements* (Nashville: Abingdon Press, 1995). See also Oden in "Confessions of a Grieving Seminary Professor," *Good News* 27, 4 (January-February, 1994): 10-13; reprinted in *In Trust* (Spring 1994): 24-25, and "Reclaiming Lost Property," a paper presented at a Consultation on the Future of The United Methodist Church, April 4-5, 1994, Atlanta, Georgia.
4. David H. Kelsey, *Between Athens and Berlin; The Theological Education Debate* (Grand Rapids, Mich.: Eerdmans, 1993), 1.
5. Based on her review of recent accreditation reports, Barbara G. Wheeler concludes that the critique of assumptions embodied in this debate has not even "invaded the consciousness of most theological educators." See footnote 2, p. 35, of Barbara G. Wheeler, "Arguments and Allies: The Yale Consultations and Recent Writings About Theological Education," *Theological Education,* vol. XXXI, no. 1 (Autumn 1994).

1. How Are They to Hear without a Preacher?

1. This story is included in my chapter "Multiple Models of Diaconal Ministry," in *Diaconal Ministry, Past, Present, & Future,* edited by Peyton G. Craighill (Providence, R.I.: North American Association for the Diaconate, 1994), 89.

2. Craig Dykstra articulates the three fundamental parts of Christian theological education as being: "(1) conducting the academic study of theology, (2) educating the church and the public in Christian faith and practice, and (3) preparing ministers for church leadership." He hopes that "theological seminaries will take the lead in envisioning and motivating a theological education in which the three strands are not left separate but in various ways interact to generate a creative synergy." See Craig Dykstra, "Looking Ahead at Theological Education," *Theological Education* 28 (Autumn 1991), 99, 104.
3. Ibid., 101, 105.
4. David H. Kelsey, *Between Athens and Berlin: The Theological Education Debate* (Grand Rapids, Mich.: Eerdmans, 1993), 223.
5. Ibid., 84-85.
6. See H. Richard Niebuhr, *The Purpose of the Church and Its Ministry* (New York: Harper and Bros., 1956), 107-10.
7. *Between Athens and Berlin*, 2, 80. Representative of the "Athens" model are the writings of Edward Farley, *The Fragility of Knowledge: Theological Education in the Church & The University* (Philadelphia: Fortress Press, 1983) and *Theologia: The Fragmentation and Unity of Theological Education* (Philadelphia: Fortress Press, 1983). A contemporary illustration of the "Berlin" model is Joseph C. Hough, Jr., and John B. Cobb, Jr., *Christian Identity and Theological Education* (Chico, Calif.: Scholars Press, 1985).
8. H. Richard Niebuhr, *The Purpose of the Church and Its Ministry*, 110. See also *Between Athens and Berlin*, 77.
9. *Between Athens and Berlin*, 92-93.
10. Neal F. Fisher, "United Methodist Seminaries and Relationships with Other Interested Parties," unpublished paper for the Association of United Methodist Theological Schools, October 3, 1991, 6.
11. For further discussion, see Donald. E. Messer, *Contemporary Images of Christian Ministry* (Nashville: Abingdon Press, 1989), 68-69.
12. Bob and Polly Holmes, "The Most Overpaid Profession in the World," pamphlet, distributed by the Department of Ministerial Education, The Methodist Church, Nashville, Tennessee. Updated with inclusive language, thanks to permission and encouragement of the authors.
13. James D. Berkley, "What Pastors Are Paid," *Leadership* (Spring 1992), 89.
14. Bob and Polly Holmes "The Most Overpaid Profession in the World."

2. A New Assault on the Seminaries

1. See Donald E. Messer, "Where Do We Go From Here?" in Donald E. Messer, *Send Me? The Itineracy in Crisis* (Nashville: Abingdon Press, 1991), 162. Duke church historian Russell E. Richey in "Evolving Patterns of Methodist Ministry," *Methodist History* 11 (October 1983), 21, declares it is totally mythological "that the ministry in the old days, the ministry we knew in our youth, the ministry that we have heard about—was esteemed, was effective, possessed authority, transformed people and congregations, was undaunted by the challenges it faced, preached with vigor and conviction, was untempted

by worldly, family, financial considerations." One generation always is tempted to idealize generations past, and discredit the present.

2. Robert L. Kelley, *Theological Education in America* (New York: George H. Doran Company, 1924), vii.

3. *The World Mission of the Church: Findings and Recommendations of the Meeting of the International Missionary Council,* Tambaram, Madras, India, December 12-29, 1938 (London, International Missionary Council, 1939), 78.

4. H. Richard Niebuhr, *The Purpose of the Church and Its Ministry* (New York: Harper & Bros., 1956), 95.

5. Thomas C. Oden, *Requiem: A Lament in Three Movements* (Nashville: Abingdon Press, 1995). See also Oden, *"Confessions of a Grieving Seminary Professor,"* Good News, 27, 4 (January/February 1994): 10-13; reprinted in *In Trust* (Spring 1994): 24-25, and "Reclaiming Lost Property," a paper presented at a Consultation on the Future of The United Methodist Church, April 4-5, 1994, Atlanta, Georgia.

6. I often have given his excellent book *Pastoral Theology: Essentials of Ministry* (San Francisco: Harper & Row, 1982) as an ordination gift.

7. From *Requiem: A Lament in Three Movements* by Thomas C. Oden. Copyright © 1995 by Abingdon Press. Used by permission, 15. Ironically, his self-description of being "out of the closet" is borrowed from language more commonly associated with the gay and lesbian experience. His condemnation of homosexuality is so strong and persistent that it seems strange he should choose to use such terminology.

8. My own ideal or approach to theological education parallels closely the model of theological education outlined by Joseph C. Hough, Jr., and John B. Cobb, Jr. in *Christian Identity and Theological Education* (Chico, Calif.: Scholars Press, 1985). A primary goal of theological education ought to be the goal of educating practical theologians who can give leadership in the context of the church's mission and ministry. Hough and Cobb emphasize that there must be a "close connection between the subject matter of courses in Bible and church history and the deepening, broadening, and clarifying of Christian identity" (p. 95). Through the study of the Bible and church history, including the neglected traditions of women and persons of color, future leaders can discover their identity as Christians. Second, they emphasize that this Christian identity must be within the context of globalization. This is not merely instruction but the "presence of a multiethnic, multicultural student body and faculty" with special emphasis on the Two-thirds World (p. 104). Third, theology and ethics must help "students think globally as Christians about the issues of the day" (p. 105). Practical theologians must be practical Christian thinkers, relating faith to action. Fourth, church and seminary must encourage "reflective practitioners" in parishes (p. 127).

9. Paul Wilkes, "The Hands That Would Shape Our Souls," *The Atlantic Monthly* (December 1990), 59-88, and Timothy C. Morgan, "Re-engineering the Seminary," *Christianity Today* (October 24, 1994), 74-78, and *God's Fierce Whimsy* (New York: The Pilgrim Press, 1985), edited by Katie G. Cannon and others known as The Mud Flower Collective.

10. Thomas C. Oden believes his book is "essentially a lament for a friend, not a diatribe against an enemy" (p. 20). *Webster's New Collegiate Dictionary,* however, defines *lament* as mourning aloud, "crying out in grief," or simply a complaint, while a *diatribe* consists of "bitter and abusive speech or writing." He may have intended to write a lament, but instead he produced a diatribe.
11. Oden, *Requiem,* 18, 25, and 54.
12. Cornel West, *Keeping Faith: Philosophy and Race in America* (New York: Routledge, 1993), 210.
13. David H. Kelsey, *To Understand God Truly: What's Theological About a Theological School* (Louisville: Westminster/John Knox Press, 1992), 22-24.
14. Oden, *Requiem,* 34.
15. Ibid., 34.
16. Ibid., 72.
17. Ibid., 40.
18. Ibid., 57 and 35.
19. Reference is made in 1993 data from The Association of Theological Schools in the United States and Canada supplied by Gail Buchwalter King, October 3, 1994.
20. Lovett H. Weems, Jr., "We Are Christians," *In Trust* (Spring 1994), 27.
21. Oden, *Requiem,* 37.
22. Ibid., 109 ff.
23. Ibid., 53 and 67.
24. Ibid., 73.
25. Ibid., 102-103.
26. Ibid., 62.
27. Ibid., 54.
28. Ibid., 37.
29. Ibid., 39.
30. Ibid., 40.
31. Ibid., 39.
32. Glenn T. Miller, "Not Sound or Accurate," *In Trust* (Spring 1994), 26.
33. Oden, *Requiem,* 64-65.
34. Neal F. Fisher, "Intemperate Condemning," *In Trust* (Spring 1994), 25.
35. Oden, *Requiem,* 38.
36. Ibid.
37. Ibid.
38. Ibid., 43.
39. Ibid., 22.
40. Ibid., 44.
41. Ibid., 24. Here Oden says he uses humor "as an instrument of grace." In the foreword former Lutheran pastor, now a Roman Catholic priest, Richard John Neuhaus, describes Oden's book as "rollickingly funny."
42. Ibid., 46.
43. See May 19, 1994 letter signed by Marie A. Burger, President of the Drew Theological Alumni Association. Reference is made particularly to an August 19, 1993 article in *Christianity Today* by Oden.

44. Catherine Keller, "Inventing the Goddess," *The Christian Century* (April 6, 1994), 341-42.
45. F. Thomas Trotter, foreword to *Ministerial Education in the American Methodist Movement* by Gerald O. McCulloh, (Nashville: United Methodist Board of Higher Education and Ministry, 1980), xii-xiii. See also 243-51.
46. Oden, *Requiem,* 141.
47. Ibid.
48. Ibid., 147-148.
49. Ibid., 93ff.
50. Ibid., 135.
51. Ibid., 47.
52. Ibid., 68.
53. Ibid., 61.
54. Ibid., 78.
55. Ibid., 76.
56. Ibid., 76, 135.
57. Ibid., 107.
58. Charles M. Wood, *Vision and Discernment* (Atlanta: Scholars Press, 1985), 95.

3. A New Vision of the Seminaries

1. Lynn White, Jr. in "The Changing Canons of Our Culture," in White, ed., *Frontiers of Knowledge: in the Study of Man* (New York: Harper and Bros., 1956), 302.
2. Ibid.
3. David B. Barrett, "Annual Statistics Table on Global Mission: 1994," *International Bulletin of Missionary Research* (January 1994), 25.
4. Average A.T.S. seminaries, however, "are still overwhelmingly white and male communities. As of 1989, there were more than twice as many men as women in M.Div. programs. African American students, men and women combined, amounted to less than 7.3 percent of the total student population. In size, theological schools are still more like primary schools in white neighborhoods that discourage the education of women than they are like modern graduate professional institutions in an open and pluralistic society," concludes David H. Kelsey, *To Understand God Truly: What's Theological About a Theological School* (Louisville: Westminster/John Knox Press, 1992), 19.
5. Don S. Browning, "Globalization and the Task of Theological Education in North America," *Theological Education,* vol. XXIII, no. 1 (Autumn 1976): 43-44. See also Donald E. Messer, *A Conspiracy of Goodness: Contemporary Images of Christian Mission* (Nashville: Abingdon Press, 1992), 34 ff.
6. See Bengt Sundkler, *The Christian Ministry in Africa* (London: S.C.M., 1960), 304. See also F. Ross Kinsler, ed., *Ministry by the People: Theological Education by Extension* (Maryknoll, N.Y.: Orbis Books, 1983) for a global survey of theological education programs. An earlier work edited by Ralph D. Winter, *Theological Education by Extension* (South Pasadena, Calif.: William Carey Library, 1969) should be noted.

7. Max L. Stackhouse, *Apologia: Contextualization, Globalization, and Mission in Theological Education* (Grand Rapids, Mich.: Eerdmans, 1988), 209.

8. Robert A. Evans, foreword to *Jesus Weeps: Global Encounters on Our Doorstep* by Harold J. Recinos (Nashville: Abingdon Press, 1992), 10.

9. Keith R. Bridston, *Mission, Myth and Reality* (New York: Friendship Press, 1965), 33.

10. Evans in Recinos, *Jesus Weeps*, 11.

11. Recinos, *Jesus Weeps*, 17.

12. See Tex Sample, *Blue Collar Ministry* (Nashville: Abingdon Press, 1984); *Hard Living People & Mainstream Christians* (Nashville: Abingdon Press, 1993); and *Ministry in an Oral Culture: Living with Will Rogers, Uncle Remus & Minnie Pearl* (Louisville: Westminster/John Knox Press, 1940).

13. Roy I. Sano, "Globalization in Theological Education," *Quarterly Review* 11/1 (1991), 86.

14. Robert J. Schreiter, *Constructing Local Theologies* (London: S.C.M. Press, 1985), 3.

15. Hans Küng, *The Council in Action* (New York: Sheed and Ward, 1963), 259.

16. Frederick K. Kirschenmann, "Rural Community's Challenge to Theological Education," unpublished paper presented to the regional consultation of the Minnesota Consortium of Theological Schools, December 4, 1992, 5, 23.

17. Aloysius Pieris, S.J., *An Asian Theology of Liberation* (Maryknoll, N.Y.: Orbis Books, 1988), 63.

18. Schreiter, *Constructing Local Theologies*, 29.

19. Emilio Castro, foreword to *Ministry by the People: Theological Education by Extension*, ed. F. Ross Kinsler (Maryknoll, N.Y.: Orbis Books, 1983), ix-xi.

20. See Sam Amirtham and S. Wesley Ariarajah, *Ministerial Formation in a Multifaith Milieu* (Geneva: World Council of Churches, 1986).

21. Statistics reported by Gail Buchwalter King, "Trends in Seminary Education, 1987-1992," in *Yearbook of American and Canadian Churches, 1993*, ed. Kenneth B. Bedell (Nashville: Abingdon Press, 1993), 262-63.

22. 1993 data from The Association of Theological Schools in the United States and Canada supplied by Gail Buchwalter King, October 3, 1994. A.T.S. membership in 1993–94 was 219 and in 1994–95, it was 226.

23. Data from *Fact Book on Theological Education, 1972–73*, and *Fact Book on Theological Education, 1992–1993*, Association of Theological Schools in the United States and Canada.

24. Statistics received from Gail Buchwalter King, Associate Director, The Association of Theological Schools in the United States and Canada, October, 1994.

25. *Fact Book on Theological Education, 1993–94* (Pittsburgh: The Association of Theological Schools in the United States and Canada, 1994), 82. Also see "ATS Enrollment by Age and Gender—Fall 1993," *ATS Colloquy*, vol. III, no. 2 (November/December 1994), 10.

26. *Fact Book on Theological Education, 1993–94*, 82.

27. The average age of United Methodist seminary students in 1992 was 35 years old versus 25 years old in 1968. Statistics are from the Division of Ordained

Ministry, General Board of Higher Education and Ministry, The United Methodist Church, Nashville, Tennessee.

28. Donald Senior and Timothy Weber, "What Is the Character of Curriculum, Formation, and Cultivation of Ministerial Leadership in the Good Theological School?" *Theological Education*, vol. XXX, no. 2 (Spring 1994), 26.

29. Carnegie Samuel Calian, "Emerging Trends Among Seminaries," *Seminary Development News*, January, 1994, 3.

30. For further discussion, see *Caught in the Crossfire: Helping Christians Debate Homosexuality*, ed. Sally B. Geis and Donald E. Messer (Nashville: Abingdon Press, 1994).

31. Marjorie Hewitt Suchocki, "A Learned Ministry?" *Quarterly Review* (Summer 1993), 4-5.

32. Anthony Ruger and Barbara G. Wheeler, "Deeper in Debt: Are Seminary Students Borrowing Too Much?" *The Christian Century* (February 2-9, 1994), 101.

4. Theological Education as a Subversive Activity

1. The most recent example within the Southern Baptist Convention was the firing of Russell H. Dilday as president of Southwestern Baptist Theological Seminary, Fort Worth, Texas, in March of 1994. The Southwestern Board issued a statement saying he was dismissed because of "doctrinal and policy differences." This incident was only the latest in a series since the fundamentalist majority within the Southern Baptist Convention "began its step-by-step purge of its critics" in 1989. See "Board Fires Veteran Seminary Chief," *In Trust* (Spring 1994), 20.

2. Donald E. Messer, *Contemporary Images of Christian Ministry* (Nashville: Abingdon Press, 1989), and *A Conspiracy of Goodness: Contemporary Images of Christian Mission* (Nashville: Abingdon Press, 1994).

3. Walter Brueggemann, *Engage/Social Action* (December 1985).

4. Desmond M. B. Tutu, "God's Kingdom of Righteousness," sermon at World Methodist Council, *Proceedings of the Fifteenth World Methodist Conference*, July 23-29, 1986, Nairobi, Kenya, ed. Joe Hale (Waynesville, N.C.: The World Methodist Council, 1987), 186.

5. Rigoberta Menchu, *I, Rigoberta Menchu, An Indian Woman in Guatemala*, ed. Elisabeth Burgos-Debray, trans. Ann Wright (London: Verso, 1984), 131-33.

6. Personal correspondence with Ms. Joyce Hill, United Methodist General Board of Global Ministries, 1993.

7. Delwin Brown, *Boundaries of Our Habitations: Tradition and Theological Construction* (Albany, N.Y.: State University of New York Press, 1994), 19. Reference is to William A. Clebsch, *Christianity in European History* (New York: Oxford University Press, 1979).

8. Julia Esquivel, "They Have Threatened Us with Resurrection," in her book *Threatened with Resurrection* (Elgin, Ill.: The Brethren Press, 1982), 59-63.

9. Jurgen Moltmann, *Religion, Revolution, and the Future* (New York: Scribner's, 1969), 121.

10. This vision of theological education is related to the literature of the Mud Flower Collective in Katie Cannon and others, *God's Fierce Whimsy* (New York: The Pilgrim Press, 1985). These feminist theologians emphasize diversity and pluralism. They recognize the inevitability of conflict and controversy. The unity of harmonious structure doesn't exist but people are committed to a method of listening and speaking to one another. As David H. Kelsey in *Between Athens and Berlin: The Theological Education Debates* (Grand Rapids, Mich.: Eerdmans, 1993, 147) remarks: "Such theological education would ideally have the unity of a vigorous ongoing, multi-party, tension-ridden conversation, not the unity of a harmonious structure."

11. For further discussion, see James M. Wall, "What Is Sexual Harassment?" *The Christian Century* (April 13, 1994), 371-72. Also see Courtney Leatherman in *The Chronicle of Higher Education* (March 16, 1994).

12. Daniel Berrigan and Robert Coles, *The Geography of Faith* (Boston: Beacon Press, 1971), 82.

13. "A Statement of Educational Purposes," The Iliff School of Theology, January, 1977, 7-8.

14. G. Bromley Oxnam, *I Protest* (New York: Harper and Bros., 1954), 16-17.

5. The Seminary as a Redemptive Community

1. Sam Keen writes in *Hymns to an Unknown God* (New York: Bantam, 1994), 69 that "in theory we are believers; it is only in practice that we are atheists."

2. F. Thomas Trotter, *Loving God With One's Mind* (Nashville: United Methodist Board of Higher Education and Ministry, 1987), 24.

3. Ibid.

4. Robert F. Kennedy, cited in Arthur M. Schlesinger, Jr., *Robert Kennedy and His Times* (Boston: Houghton Mifflin, 1978), 914.

5. For extended discussion of new images of mission and ministry, see Donald E. Messer, *Contemporary Images of Christian Ministry* (Nashville: Abingdon, 1989) and *A Conspiracy of Goodness: Contemporary Images of Christian Mission* (Nashville: Abingdon Press, 1992).

6. Theologian Edward Farley envisioned the ultimate goal of theological seminaries as "redemption." He saw the seminaries as seeking to be "redemptive communities." See Edward Farley, *Theologia: The Fragmentation and Unity of Theological Education* (Philadelphia: Fortress Press, 1983), 176. For the Mud Flower Collective, "the fundamental goal of theological education must be the doing of justice." For them, the heart of an intellectual love of God and neighbor necessitates doing justice. See Katie G. Cannon and others, *God's Fierce Whimsy* (New York: The Pilgrim Press, 1986), 204. For a critical discussion, see David H. Kelsey, *Between Athens and Berlin: The Theological Education Debate* (Grand Rapids, Mich.: Eerdmans, 1993), 143 ff.

7. Henri J. M. Nouwen, *Gracias! A Latin American Journal* (San Francisco: Harper & Row, 1983), 18.

8. Taylor Branch, *Parting the Waters: America in the King Years, 1954–63* (New York: Simon and Schuster, 1988), xii.

9. Aaron Sachs, "HIV/AIDS Cases Rising Steadily," in Lester R. Brown, Hal Kane, and David Malin Roodman, *Vital Signs 1994* (New York, Worldwatch Institute, 1994), 102.

10. Martin E. Marty, "Tears," *The Christian Century* (November 30, 1988), 1111.

11. Avery Dulles, *Models of the Church* (Garden City, N.Y.: Doubleday, 1978), 170.

12. Cited by Rabbi Kirschner in his Kol Nidre sermon during the High Holy Days of 1985.

13. Donald W. Shriver cited by Craig Dykstra in *Theological Education* (August 1991), 96.

14. M. Thomas Thangaraj, "Theological Education in the United States: A View from the Periphery," *Theological Education* 28 (Spring 1992), 17.

6. Publish *and* Parish

1. Philip S. Keane and Melanie A. May, "What Is the Character of Teaching, Learning, and the Scholarly Task in the Good Theological School?" *Theological Education*, vol. XXX no. 2 (Spring 1994), 39.

2. The above two paragraphs are from Donald E. Messer, *Contemporary Images of Christian Ministry* (Nashville: Abingdon Press, 1989), 155-56.

3. Ironically, ten years later I was elected president of the same college!

4. Donald E. Messer, " 'Rescuing' the Cult Member," *Christian Century* 99 (February 24, 1982), 213-15.

5. Richard J. Mouw, "Faculty as Scholars and Teachers," *Theological Education* (Autumn 1991), 77-78.

6. Reprinted from *PC Magazine*, December 7, 1993, in *Context*, vol. 26 no. 3 (February 1, 1994), 6.

7. Rudolf Bultmann, *Jesus Christ and Mythology* (New York: Macmillan, 1981).

8. Henri J. M. Nouwen, "Silence," *Catalyst* tape, vol. 13, no. 2, 1980.

9. Ibid.

7. Prepare a Superhighway for Our God

1. See Joseph Blenkinsopp, *Harper's Bible Commentary* ed. James L. Mays (San Francisco: Harper San Francisco, 1988), 573-74.

2. Peter H. Lewis, "Here's to the Techies Who Lunch," *The New York Times,* August 27, 1994, Y17.

3. David Gonzales, "The Computer Age Bids Religious World to Enter," *The New York Times,* July 24, 1994, 12.

4. Arthur J. Moen, "The Bible Software Search," *Christian Ministry* (March-April 1994), 21.

5. T. S. Eliot, "Choruses from 'The Rock,' " in *T. S. Eliot: The Complete Poems and Plays* (New York: Harcourt, Brace Jovanovich, 1952).

6. Gonzales, *The New York Times,* 12.

7. David Gonzales, "Some Cyberspace Users Singing, 'Gimmie That On-Line Religion,' " *The Denver Post,* 10A.

8. Gonzales, *The New York Times,* 12.

9. Ibid.

10. See *Changing the Process of Teaching and Learning: Essays by Notre Dame Faculty* (University of Notre Dame Education Media, 1994), 53-59.

11. See J. Patrick Michaels, Jr. in *Religion, Television and the Information Superhighway,* compiled by Robert Lewis Shayon and Nash Cox (Philadelphia: Waymark Press, 1994).

12. Excerpt from Charles M. Oliver, in ibid., 69.

13. Augustine quoted by Robert McAfee Brown in *Context,* vol. 24, no. 3 (February 1, 1992), 3.

14. This quotation is often attributed to Robert F. Kennedy. In fact it was said by Shaw.

15. From *The Poetry of Robert Frost* ed. Edward Connery Lathem (Orlando, Fla.: Holt, Rinehart and Winston, 1979).

BIBLIOGRAPHY

Amirtham, Sam and S. Wesley Ariarajah, ed. *Ministerial Formation in a Multifaith Milieu.* Geneva: World Council of Churches, 1986.

Cannon, Katie G. and others (The Mud Flower Collective). *God's Fierce Whimsy: Christian Feminism and Theological Education.* New York: Pilgrim Press, 1985.

Carter, I. Carter and others, "Christian Feminists Speak," *Theological Education* 20 (Spring 1984).

Dykstra, Craig, "Looking Ahead at Theological Education," *Theological Education* 28 (Autumn 1991).

Fact Book on Theological Education, The Association of Theological Schools.

Farley, Edward. *The Fragility of Knowledge: Theological Education in the Church & the University.* Philadelphia: Fortress Press, 1988.

————. *Theologia: The Fragmentation and Unity of Theological Education.* Philadelphia: Fortress Press, 1983.

Fisher, Neal F. *Truth and Tradition: A Conversation About the Future of United Methodist Theological Education.* Nashville: Abingdon Press, 1995.

Gustafson, James M., "Priorities in Theological Education," *Theological Education* 23 (Supplement 1987).

Hessel, Dieter T. *Theological Education for Social Ministry.* New York: The Pilgrim Press, 1988.

Hough, Joseph C., Jr. and John B. Cobb, Jr. *Christian Identity and Theological Education.* Chico, Calif.: Scholars Press, 1985.

Kelsey, David H. *Between Athens and Berlin: The Theological Education Debate.* Grand Rapids, Mich.: Eerdmans, 1993.

————. *To Understand God Truly: What's Theological About a Theological School.* Louisville: Westminster/John Knox, 1992.

Kinsler, F. Ross, ed. *Ministry by the People.* Maryknoll, N.Y.: Orbis Books, 1983.

Kitagawa, Joseph Mitsuo, ed. *Religious Studies, Theological Studies, and the University-Divinity School.* Atlanta: Scholars Press, 1992.

Larsen, Ellis and James Shopshire, "A Profile of Contemporary Seminarians," *Theological Education* 24 (Spring 1988).

McCulloh, Gerald O. *Ministerial Education in the American Methodist Movement.* Nashville: United Methodist Board of Higher Education and Ministry, 1980.

Niebuhr, H. Richard. *The Purpose of the Church and Its Ministry: Reflections on the Aims of Theological Education.* New York: Harper and Bros., 1956.

Niebuhr, H. Richard, Daniel Day Williams and James M. Gustafson. *The Advancement of Theological Education.* New York: Harper and Bros., 1957.

Oden, Thomas C. *Requiem: A Lament in Three Movements.* Nashville: Abingdon Press, 1995.

Morgan, Timothy C., "Re-Engineering the Seminary," *Christianity Today* (October 24, 1994).

Mouw, Richard J., "Faculty as Scholars and Teachers," *Theological Education* 28 (Autumn 1991).

Richey, Russell E., ed. *Ecumenical & Interreligious Perspectives: Globalization in Theological Education.* Nashville: Quarterly Review Books, 1992.

Schner, George P. *Education for Ministry: Reform and Renewal in Theological Education.* Kansas City, Mo.: Sheed & Ward, 1993.

Stackhouse, Max L. *Apologia: Contextualization, Globalization, and Mission in Theological Education.* Grand Rapids, Mich.: Eerdmans, 1988.

Thangaraj, M. Thomas, "Theological Education in the United States: A View from the Periphery," *Theological Education* 28 (Spring 1992).

Theological Education, "The Good Theological School," vol. XXX, no. 2 (Spring 1994). This journal of the Association of Theological Schools in the United States and Canada is published semiannually in Pittsburgh, Pennsylvania.

West, Cornel, "The Crisis in Theological Education," in *Prophetic Fragments.* Grand Rapids, Mich.: Eerdmans, 1988.

Wheeler, Barbara G., and Edward Farley, eds. *Shifting Boundaries: Contextual Approaches to the Structure of Theological Education.* Louisville: Westminster/John Knox, 1991.

Wilkes, Paul, "The Hands That Would Shape Our Souls," *The Atlantic Monthly* (December 1990).

Wood, Charles M. *Vision and Discernment: An Orientation in Theological Study.* Chico, Calif.: Scholars Press, 1985.

INDEX